# The Village: Russian Impressions

## AMERICANS IN REVOLUTIONARY RUSSIA

Vol. 1
Albert Rhys Williams, *Through the Russian Revolution*,
edited by William Benton Whisenhunt (2016)

Vol. 2
Princess Julia Cantacuzène, Countess Spéransky, *Russian People: Revolutionary Recollections*, edited by Norman E. Saul (2016)

Vol. 3
Ernest Poole, *The Village: Russian Impressions*, edited by Norman E. Saul (2017)

Vol. 4
John Reed, *Ten Days That Shook the World*,
edited by William Benton Whisenhunt (2017)

Vol. 5
Louise Bryant, *Six Red Months in Russia: An Observer's Account of Russia Before and During the Proletarian Dictatorship*, edited by Lee A. Farrow (2017)

### Series General Editors
Norman E. Saul and William Benton Whisenhunt

# The Village: Russian Impressions

Ernest Poole

Edited and Introduction by
Norman E. Saul

ANTHEM PRESS

Anthem Press
An imprint of Wimbledon Publishing Company
*www.anthempress.com*

First published by Slavica Publishers, Indiana University, USA, 2017

This edition first published in UK and USA 2026
by ANTHEM PRESS
75–76 Blackfriars Road, London SE1 8HA, UK
or PO Box 9779, London SW19 7ZG, UK
and
244 Madison Ave #116, New York, NY 10016, USA

Copyright © 2026 Norman E. Saul editorial matter and selection;
individual chapters © individual contributors

The moral right of the authors has been asserted.

All rights reserved. Without limiting the rights under copyright reserved above,
no part of this publication may be reproduced, stored or introduced into
a retrieval system, or transmitted, in any form or by any means
(electronic, mechanical, photocopying, recording or otherwise),
without the prior written permission of both the copyright
owner and the above publisher of this book.

*British Library Cataloguing-in-Publication Data*
A catalogue record for this book is available from the British Library.

*Library of Congress Cataloging-in-Publication Data*
A catalog record for this book has been requested.

ISBN-13: 978-1-83999-728-0 (Hbk)
ISBN-10: 1-83999-728-1 (Hbk)

ISBN-13: 978-1-83999-729-7 (Pbk)
ISBN-10: 1-83999-729-X (Pbk)

Cover design by Tracey Theriault.
Cover image courtesy of Library of Congress, Prints and Photographs Division

This title is also available as an eBook.

# CONTENTS

Editor's Introduction      ix
    Norman E. Saul

# THE VILLAGE

Chapter 1      1

Chapter 2      35

Chapter 3      55

Chapter 4      77

Chapter 5      99

Index      117

# ILLUSTRATIONS

"The Dark People"                                               Figure 1

Market Day                                                      Figure 2

Peasant Veterinary Doctors                                      Figure 3

# EDITOR'S INTRODUCTION

### Norman E. Saul

Unlike most of the American eyewitnesses to the Russian Revolution, Ernest Poole (1880–1950) was already an accomplished professional writer well known to the American public.[1] He had also experienced Russia in revolution in 1905, had studied the language and the country's history, and had read many Russian literary works, especially those of Leo Tolstoy, Ivan Turgenev, and Maxim Gorky. He thus had an advantage over those who were new to the land and its people. Furthermore, in contrast to many of his compatriots, Poole was convinced that the real Russia was to be found in the countryside, among the peasants, and concentrated his time and efforts in understanding what was happening there.

Poole was born and raised in an upper-class neighborhood on Chicago's north side, near the corner of Erie and what is now Michigan Avenue. His father, of Dutch background (the family's original name was Vanderpoehl), came from upstate New York, and had moved west, first to Wisconsin and then to Chicago. Abram Poole served in the Union Army, marching with Sherman through Georgia, and worked his way up the ranks of the Chicago Board of Trade to become a leading "member," often acting as broker for Philip Danforth Armour of meat packing fame.[2] Ernest Poole and his seven siblings (four sisters and three brothers) grew up in a large Victorian house that he remembered as bustling with activity and visitors, in particular during the World's Fair of 1893. The family spent its summers at a beach house in Lake Forest.[3]

The young Ernest learned early to escape this crowd by roaming with a gang of other boys through a nearby slum of shanties and tents occupying a Lake Michigan

---

[1] Ernest Poole was unrelated to two other Pooles who were prominent in Russia during this period: DeWitt Clinton Poole, who served as American consul general in Moscow in 1917–18, and General Frederick C. Poole, British commander of the interventionist forces in the north of Russia in 1918–19.

[2] Ernest Poole, *Giants Gone: Men Who Made Chicago* (New York: Whittlesey House-McGraw-Hill, 1943), 107–09.

[3] Ernest Poole, *The Bridge: My Own Story* (New York: Macmillan Company, 1940), 4, 24, 32.

landfill called "the Patch."[4] These childhood explorations sparked Poole's life-long interest in the world of the lower class, whose struggles would influence much of his literary work. Poole's family milieu thus stood in sharp contrast to this other world of poverty and disease, a disconnect of which he was acutely aware as he described the high-society life of his summers at Lake Forest.

Ernest Poole received his formal education at a Chicago high school associated with the University of Chicago. In 1898 he enrolled at Princeton University, then as now one of America's leading institutions of higher education. In his autobiography Poole admits to having been an indifferent student for the first two years, more assiduous in his enjoyment of eating (and drinking) clubs than in his studies. He credits a professor of history and politics, Woodrow Wilson, for inspiring the interest in writing and social welfare to which he would devote much of his efforts in his remaining years at Princeton. Poole also succumbed at this time to the contemporary American craze for Russian literature, especially Tolstoy and Turgenev.[5]

During his college years, Poole spent summers with family and friends back in Chicago and Lake Forest. It was at this time that he met the "love of his life," Margaret Ann Winterbotham, the daughter of another leading Chicago family; they would marry in 1907.[6] In August 1902, after graduating from Princeton, he moved into the University Settlement on New York's Lower East Side.[7] This was another, and different, introduction to tenement slum life—and to Russia, since many of the people served by the Settlement were Jewish immigrants from Eastern Europe, especially from the Russian Empire, where antisemitism was at its height. Among other "residents" serving this community with shelter, food, and English-language courses were Arthur Bullard, William English Walling, Leroy Scott, Phelps Stokes, and Walter Weyl, all of whom also developed professional interests in the Russian revolutionary movement. Bullard and Walling would be among Poole's life-long friends, and Weyl would marry one of Poole's sisters, Bertha, who had also joined the social welfare movement.[8]

The University Settlement drew many of those advocating increased public support for programs assisting poor immigrants. Visiting speakers included Jane

---

[4] Ibid, 38–40.

[5] Ibid., 55, 62–66. He cites Wilson as "his favorite professor and friend," who often joined Poole and classmates for a "smoke" in their rooms. Wilson became president of the university the year Poole graduated, 1902.

[6] Ibid., 60.

[7] Founded in 1886 as the Neighborhood Guild in a basement on Forsyth Street, by 1902 it had become one of the largest and most active settlement houses, comparable to the nearby Henry Street Settlement and Hull House in Chicago. It continues to be one of the most prominent relief agencies in the city.

[8] Poole, *The Bridge*, 68–72.

Addams, Lillian Wald, Clarence Darrow, H. G. Wells, and Lincoln Steffens. Steffens encouraged Poole's initial writings about the many street boys who roamed the area. Poole also associated with Abraham Cahan, a Russian Jewish social revolutionary who edited a local socialist newspaper. Cahan and Poole attended the Jewish Theater together, stimulating the latter's study of Yiddish and interest in the Russian Jewish neighborhood.[9] Poole was soon exploring the nooks and crannies of the Lower East Side, taking notes and developing his reporting skills. His first published article, "Waifs of the Street," appeared in *McClure's Magazine* in May 1902.[10] It, together with a pamphlet about the "The Lung Block" written for the New York Charity Organization Committee, brought Poole and his concerns about street children and the crowded, disease-ridden tenements to the public eye.[11] Additional writings were assembled into his first substantial publication, *The Voice of the Street*, considered by *The Bookman* to be "a book of unusual quality."[12]

By this time Poole had moved out of University Settlement to share an apartment nearby with Fred King, a Yale graduate who had been strongly influenced by Tolstoy. They continued to roam the East Side with another friend from the Settlement, Howard Brubaker, soon to be the editor of *Colliers' Weekly*, and were frequent visitors to the Henry Street Settlement, the home of Lillian Wald and her visiting nurses. Poole later said that Wald "meant more to [him] than any other woman in social service."[13] His connections with the "settlement movement," then at its height, would be paramount for a few more years.

No doubt knowing that Poole was from Chicago, *Outlook*, a leading American progressive journal, sent him there in 1904 to cover the Stockyards Strike.[14] He immediately connected with the settlement house of the University of Chicago and with its director, Mary McDowell, a veteran of Hull House. The University of Chicago Settlement House was located near the slum area of "Packingtown," an

---

[9] Ibid., 74.

[10] Ibid., 70; Poole, "Waifs of the Street," *McClure's Magazine* 21, 1 (May 1903): 5–8.

[11] "The School of the Street," *The Youth's Companion* 77, 27 (2 July 1903): 328; "Some Plague Spots in New York: In One Block 265 Cases of Tuberculosis Were Reported in Nine Years," *New York Tribune*, 13 September 1903, A1; "Modern Medicine, Surgery and Sanitation," *Current Literature* 35, 6 (December 1903): 746. The editor is indebted to ProQuest Historical Newspapers for the newspaper and periodical citations.

[12] Ernest Poole, *The Voice of the Street: A Story of Temptation* (New York: Barnes and Company, 1906); "The Voice of the Street," review of *The Voice of the Street: A Story of Temptation*, by Ernest Poole, *The Bookman* 23, 6 (August 1906): 640.

[13] Poole, *The Bridge*, 85.

[14] Among the American liberals who were regular contributors to *Outlook* was George Kennan.

area populated mainly by Polish, Slovak, and Lithuanian immigrants.[15] If anything, conditions there were worse than those on New York's Lower East Side owing to poorer housing and increased pollution from the stockyards and meat packing plants.

Chicago, as a major industrial center, had a history of labor strife, notably the Haymarket Square Riot of 1886 and the 1894 Pullman Strike. The Stockyards Strike began in May 1904 when the packing houses (Meat Trust) offered workers a new annual contract that reduced hourly wages from eighteen and a half cents to sixteen and a half, or $7.40 for a forty-hour week, well below a living wage. Such slave-labor wages were made possible by an abundance of unemployed ready to work at any price. The strike by 60,000 unskilled and skilled workers, led by Michael Donnelly, an American Federation of Labor organizer, also had as its goal the creation of a stronger, more inclusive union, the Amalgamated Meat Cutters and Butcher Workmen of North America (AMC). Poole's sympathies were clearly with the unions, and he criticized the employers' tactics of refusing to compromise and of hiring black strikebreakers from the south. In articles he wrote jointly with William Hard, a writer for the *Chicago Tribune* who was also associated with Hull House, Poole lamented the inability of workers of varied ethnic backgrounds to unite.[16]

Poole spent the miserably hot Chicago summer in the company of others depressed by the union's failure. In addition to Hard and McDowell, he met John Commons, a University of Wisconsin professor of economics, and writer Upton Sinclair, both of whom were sympathetic to the plight of the workingman. Commons and Sinclair may have influenced Poole's most significant writing on the strike, a semifictional autobiography of a Lithuanian immigrant worker, "From Lithuania to the Chicago Stockyards—An Autobiography."[17] At about this same time, Poole's Chicago family began to break up with the death of his mother, the marriage of two sisters, and the departure of his younger brother Abram to study art in Munich.[18]

Meanwhile, in February 1904 war began in the Far East with the surprise attack by Japan on Vladivostok and Port Arthur. The chief cause was a clash of interests of Russia and Japan, the two new imperial powers in the region, aggravated by

---

[15] The University of Chicago Settlement was founded in 1895 by William Rainey Harper, founding president of the university, to provide service to the city and to provide an activity for faculty wives. As with the University Settlement in New York, it continues as a major welfare agency to this day. "University of Chicago Settlement," The Social Welfare History Project, socialwelfarehistory.com/settlement-houses/university-chicago-settlement (accessed 22 February 2017).

[16] Ernest Poole, "The Meat Strike," *The Independent*, 28 July 1904, 179. See also William Hard and Ernest Poole, "The Stock Yards Strike," *Outlook*, 13 August 1904, 884.

[17] Ernest Poole, "From Lithuania to the Chicago Stockyards—An Autobiography," *The Independent*, 4 August 1904.

[18] Poole, *The Bridge*, 102–03.

Russia's lease of Port Arthur on the southern tip of Manchuria. Another factor in the growing Russian presence in what many in Japan considered their sphere of interest was the construction of the Trans-Siberian Railroad. Russia's rash decision to send the Baltic Fleet to the Pacific ended in disaster at the Battle of Tsushima in May 1905. The fall of Port Arthur and the necessity of supplying troops and arms to a distant front placed additional strain on a sprawling empire already in the throes of rapid industrialization. The result was revolution, which began with the massacre of peaceful demonstrators in St. Petersburg's Palace Square on "Bloody Sunday," January 22, 1905. Ernest Poole hastened to the offices of the *Outlook* begging for a new assignment—Russia—which he received.

Packing in a rush, he was aboard ship by January 28. After brief stops in Paris and Berlin, he arrived in St. Petersburg in mid-February, carrying funds donated for progressive and radical causes by Russian exiles in Europe. He delivered the money to Harold Williams, correspondent of the *Manchester Guardian*, who provided him with an orientation to the city.[19] Poole was soon busy conducting interviews and writing articles for *Outlook*, identified only as "special correspondent in Russia." His first report, "St. Petersburg is Quiet!", dated February 18 and published a month later, described his settling in with a Russian family and beginning his study of Russian, and discussed his interviews with public officials.[20] The sixth article in the series, published in late May, finally revealed Poole's identity; the delay was due to the journal's fear that its correspondent might be expelled, as George Kennan had been a few years earlier.[21] One of Poole's best portraits of Russia during the 1905 revolution was "Two Russian Soldiers," based on interviews conducted on a train.[22]

He also wrote about meeting Juvenale (Iuvenalii) Tarasov, who was to be featured in the books Poole wrote in 1917, especially *The Village*. Tarasov is described as a large man educated in chemistry at St. Petersburg University who had traveled abroad and had some proficiency in English. He accompanied Poole on his trips into the Russian countryside.[23] Tarasov also served as guide on excursions to Ukraine and the Caucasus, where they met a Cossack who had spent four years touring with Buffalo Bill's Wild West Show. After being hounded by the police while visiting Tiflis

---

[19] Ibid., 115–19. Williams (1876–1928), a noted linguist from New Zealand, was closely associated with the Constitutional Democratic Party through his marriage in 1906 to Ariadna Tyrkova (1869–1962), one of its founders. They fled Russia in 1918. Ariadna Tyrkova-Williams emigrated to the United States in 1951.

[20] *Outlook*, 18 March 1905, 680–91.

[21] Ernest Poole, "The Peasant and the War," *Outlook*, 27 May 1905, 219–30.

[22] Ernest Poole, "Two Russian Soldiers," *Outlook*, 2 September 1905, 21.

[23] See Ernest Poole, "Russian Hamlet," *Outlook*, 29 April 1905, 135–40; Poole, "Russian Villager," *Outlook*, 13 May 1905, 113–18.

and Vladikavkaz, Poole felt the need to leave the region, reluctantly, as he had been charmed by the beauty of the landscape and the attractive women.[24]

Poole did not return directly to America. Instead he spent a month in London, writing during the day and visiting theaters in the evening, often accompanied by Walling.[25] Then he went to Paris, where he met Brubaker, Bullard, and King, who joined him for hiking in the Swiss Alps. From there he traveled to Munich to visit his artist brother before returning to Chicago in October, where he wrote a touching portrait of a Russian peasant girl for *Independent* and an extended description of his trip through the Caucasus for *Outlook*.[26]

By early 1906 Poole was back in New York. He found the old settlement group drifting apart. Walling and Bullard had left for Russia, but he joined Brubaker and Weyl in an apartment on Fifth Avenue, near Washington Square, where they formed the "A Club," which was devoted to discussions of theater. Poole's turn in this direction was probably influenced by his exposure to theater in Europe, though he gives particular credit to the appearance of a Russian drama company in New York headed by the well-known Russian actor Pavel Ivanovich Orlenev (1869–1932).[27]

---

[24] Poole, *The Bridge*, 167. Poole had written in a letter to his father that he might stay in the Caucasus and marry a local girl.

[25] Out of money by this time, Poole wired his father, who sent money, relieved to know that his son had left the Caucasus.

[26] Ernest Poole, "Dounya," *The Independent*, 26 October 1905, 974; Poole, "With the Caucasian Revolutionists," *Outlook*, 18 November 1905, 653. Altogether Poole published over 200 printed pages on Russia in 1905, the equivalent of a book.

[27] Poole, *The Bridge*, 190; "Orlenev," *St. Petersburg Encyclopedia*, www.encspb.ru (accessed 13 March 2017). Orlenev and his wife, Alla Nazimova (1879–1945), a Moscow Art Theater actress, performed there briefly in 1904 and were encouraged to return with a company of actors to produce a repertoire of Russian and other plays. The "St. Petersburg Players" arrived in the spring of 1905, the first such visit to the United States by a Russian touring company. They scored a rave review, especially for Nazimova, at their opening at the Herald Square Theater ("A Russian Play," *New-York Tribune*, 24 March 1905, 7; "Paul Orleneff, the Russian Actor: His Aspirations and Ideals," *New York Times*, 2 April 1905, SM3). Orlenev's forte was playing Oswald in Henrik Ibsen's *Ghosts* and Raskolnikov in an adaptation of Fedor Dostoevsky's *Crime and Punishment* ("Russian Actors in "Ghosts," *New York Times*, 11 June 1905, 20).

In November 1905 Orlenov rented a small theater on the Lower East Side, the "Russian Lyceum," no doubt aware of a potential audience of Russian Jews, as all the performances were in Russian ("Russian Theater Opened," *New York Times*, 4 November 1905, 9). One of the most popular presentations was Russian playwright Evgenii Chirikov's *The Chosen People*, a dramatic depiction of the April 1903 pogrom in Kishinev, which had been banned in Russia. *The Chosen People* together with productions of works by Ibsen, Chekhov, and others attracted a good deal of attention, despite being performed in Russian. The Lyceum, however, ran into problems, and finally the city fire marshal ordered it closed. Still, boosted by the much publicized visit of Maxim Gorky and a $10,000 aid fund, the Russian players continued well into 1906 and toured in Chicago and Boston as well.

Poole, apparently supported by his father, spent much of the summer of 1906 tramping in the Alps with his brother Abram and Bullard. In Lucerne and Interlaken they were joined by the young woman he had wooed in Chicago—Margaret Ann Winterbotham. They apparently returned to the United States together, as he notes that he begged her to marry him "all the way across the Atlantic." The wedding in the Winterbotham home in Chicago on February 12, 1907, was a modest affair, with Poole's older brother Ralph as best man and the bride's younger sister Katherine as bridesmaid.[28] After a brief reception they departed by train for New York and a two-month honeymoon in Europe, some of it in his brother Abram's apartment in Munich. Back in America they spent the summer in New Hampshire, and in the fall rented a small house in Greenwich Village.[29]

The new Mrs. Poole reinforced her husband's commitments to social progress by being active in such causes as women's suffrage and Mabel Kittredge's campaign for school lunches in New York City public schools. A highlight of the latter occurred in 1913 when Margaret Poole escorted Theodore Roosevelt to Public School 95 in Greenwich Village for a luncheon of bean soup and egg sandwich (one cent each).[30] She also served as president of the Woman's City Club of New York, while bearing three children during the first five years of marriage and being a firm supporter of her husband's career.

Meanwhile, Poole devoted most of his attention to writing plays, a total of eleven (including two with Harriet Ford), only two of which were actually produced.[31] *None So Blind* opened in New Haven on January 29, 1910, and moved to the Hackett Theater in New York on February 3.[32] *None So Blind* told the story of a construction engineer who goes blind in the middle of a bridge construction project and who then has an operation to restore his sight but who pretends to still be blind in order to uncover the betrayals of his wife and a rival engineer.[33] The second play, *A Man's Friends*, had a better reception as a "drama of real merit."[34] Opening in March 1913, it depicted an honest district attorney's fight against a corrupt political boss who relies on duping

---

[28] "In the Society World," *Chicago Daily Tribune*, 13 February 1907, 18.

[29] Poole, *The Bridge*, 179–81.

[30] "Colonel Eats 2-Cent Meal: >It Was Bully'" *New York Tribune*, April 16, 1913, 11.

[31] Poole, *The Bridge*, 192. Harriet Ford was more successful with sixteen Broadway productions and several film scripts. Apparently a third play with Ford, *Take Your Medicine*, was produced in 1916 in revised form; at least one major reviewer considered it Poole's best play. George S. Kaufman, "Broadway and Elsewhere," *New York Tribune*, 10 December 1916, 31; Truman Frederick Keefer, *Ernest Poole* (New York: Twayne, 1966), 37.

[32] "Theatrical Notes," *New York Tribune*, 29 January 1910, 7.

[33] "*None So Blind*," *The Bookman* 31, 2 (April 1910): 142.

[34] "*A Man's Friends*," *New York Tribune*, 23 March 1913, 9.

his friends for support.[35] Poole also continued his journalistic career with two short, perceptive biographies.[36]

Discouraged by his limited success in the theater world, Poole turned to a larger project: writing a novel. In early 1914 he learned that his first book, *The Harbor*, had been accepted by the Macmillan publishing house. To celebrate, he and his wife dashed off to France, leaving the children with their grandmother Winterbotham. They reached Paris by May 1, where they met Bullard, who warned them of major events ahead in Europe. They went on to tour the Pyrenees and Spain, and enjoyed the flamenco craze in Paris. In June they were back in the White Mountains of New Hampshire for Poole to make some revisions to *The Harbor* and begin work on a second novel.[37] His New Hampshire summer was interrupted by a world event. Europe went to war in August 1914, and Poole once again donned his correspondent cap.

This time he knocked on the door of *The Saturday Evening Post*, for which he had recently written some short stories, and was soon on the scene—in Germany! He spent a week in Silesia with an American Red Cross unit and quickly became acquainted first-hand with the horrors of modern war. Then, back in Berlin he received permission to visit the Western Front with a group of correspondents that included John Reed, with whom he visited an army hospital located just behind the lines. Poole described buying tobacco at a shop in a French village occupied by the Germans and a superb dinner at the headquarters of General Von Falkenhayn. He was impressed by German cleanliness and ingenuity, for example, in making alcohol from sugar beets to run trucks and using crushed rock on mud to firm the roads.

Poole returned in time to see the publication of *The Harbor* in February 1915. The book received a surprisingly favorable critical and public response: "It is one of the ablest novels added to American fiction in many a year."[38] The author received laudatory letters from Theodore Roosevelt, William Allen White, William Dean Howells, Hamlin Garland, Walter Lippmann, John Reed, and others. Set in Brooklyn, *The Harbor* draws on Poole's childhood experiences in Chicago and his adventures on the New York waterfront to tell two stories: one of a wealthy family involved in the modern shipping business and the other of the dockyard and its impoverished workers. The novel laments not only the passing of beauty as graceful Yankee clippers are replaced by ugly cargo ships, but also the passing of America's hegemony at sea. Though quite popular at the time, it is not easy reading for later generations.

---

[35] "A Man's Friends," *The Bookman* 37, 3 (May 1913): 308.

[36] "Abraham Cahan," *Outlook*, 28 October 1911, 467–78; and "Brandeis," *American Magazine* 71 (February 1911): 481–93.

[37] Poole, *The Bridge*, 213–16.

[38] "Views and Reviews of Current Fiction," *New York Tribune*, 13 February 1915, 10. It was reprinted five times within a month and twenty-two times overall, as well as in several translations, including Russian (Poole, *The Bridge*, 259).

Poole's second novel, *His Family*, came out in May 1917, after being serialized by *Everybody's Magazine*, beginning in September 1916. It tells the story of a man who awakes to the memory of having promised his dying wife some years earlier that he would maintain contact with their two daughters and bring their life stories to her when he dies. He finds them proceeding with contrasting lives, one embedded in and devoted to a nuclear family, the other a principal of a school of 3,000 students — the small, intimate family contrasted with the larger social family in which we all live. *His Family* was praised as purely New York but also quite personal, as one prominent reviewer noted: "This book is chiefly to be prized as a picture of Mr. Poole's own soul—a picture that one likes to remember for heartenment and reassurance. It rewards the best that one can bring to it.... It has spiritual penetration and latitude and elevation. It is filled throughout with a deep and intimate consciousness of the reality of other souls."[39] The following year *His Family* was awarded the first Pulitzer Prize in fiction for a work that best depicts "the wholesome atmosphere of American life and the highest standard of American manners and manhood."[40]

Once again major events intervened in Poole's career—the Russian revolution of 1917 and American entry into the war. The first call for special duty came from his old friend Arthur Bullard on behalf of George Creel, who was the director of the newly created Committee on Public Information. Often dubbed the "Creel Committee," it was a controversial propaganda agency created to support the American war effort through news releases, public speeches, and film, and subsequently expanded to shore up America's allies, especially Russia. He worked at the Public Information office in New York for several weeks before Bullard convinced him to go to Russia.[41]

Poole again signed on with *The Saturday Evening Post* and arrived in Russia with a number of other journalists and exiles in May. He toured Nevsky Prospect with the United Press's William Shepherd, one of the best known American journalists in Russia at the time of the revolution.[42] Initially, Poole deliberately selected as interpreter a Bolshevik who said that nothing could stop the revolutionaries, an avowal borne out by Poole's wild experience during the armed July demonstrations,

---

[39] Lawrence Gilman, "The Book of the Month: A New York Family," *The North American Review* 205, 739 (June 1917): 946.

[40] "Columbia Awards Prizes in Letters, Art, Journalism," *New York Tribune*, 4 June 1918, B2. Some critics considered *The Harbor* better and opined that the prize represented a retrospective award for that work.

[41] Poole, *The Bridge*, 267.

[42] Most of the American "journalists" in Russia in 1917, such as Poole, John Reed, Bessie Beattie, and Donald Thompson were on temporary contracts with newspapers or journals. A few, such as Shepherd and Robert Crozier Long of the Associated Press, were permanent employees on assignment in Russia. Shepherd probably published more on Russia at the time than anyone but did not write a book.

as described in the early pages of *"The Dark People."*[43] During the July Days, Poole was reunited at last with Iuvenalii Tarasov, his friend and guide from 1905, who was once again to serve as his guide. Tarasov expressed much greater pessimism about Russia than he had at the time of the first revolution. He saw Russia "sliding into hell": Petrograd was chaotic, with demonstrations every weekend, and there was genuine fear that the Hermitage might be destroyed due to its proximity to the Winter Palace, the headquarters of the Provisional Government, which was under attack. Most of the middle and upper classes were fleeing the city. As before, Tarasov urged Poole to spend time in his village and in the Russian countryside.

Poole's reports from Russia were subsequently revised and assembled into two books, *"The Dark People": Russia's Crisis* (1918) and *The Village: Russian Impressions* (1919). *"The Dark People"* covers the first months of his stay, focusing on the view from the top and describing the urban scene. *The Village* tells of Poole's weeks-long immersion in the Russian countryside. It, rather than *"The Dark People,"* has been chosen for publication in the "Americans in Revolutionary Russia" series because in my opinion it is better written and provides a view of Russia that differs from those offered by other American observers. It also seems to have been better received, by both readers and critics, for its emphasis on character studies—impoverished landowner, school teacher, priest, midwife, artist (Tarasov's father)—and descriptions of river steamers, new school house, cooperative store, peasant bank, and an assortment of peasant huts.[44]

Back in Petrograd in September, Poole found the situation more confused than ever, with faction fighting faction and the wealthy fleeing. He and Bullard were convinced that American aid for Russia was crucial to winning the war, regardless of who was in power. With the help of a Red Cross volunteer from the Swift meat packing family of Chicago, Poole succeeded in obtaining a berth on a special American Red Cross car on the Trans-Siberian Railroad. Tarasov saw him off, more depressed than ever about Russia's future. Poole, in no hurry to get home after the long trip across Siberia, spent a few days each in Peking and Tokyo, before boarding a ship bound for the United States. He stopped in Chicago to visit a sister and then proceeded to New

---

[43] Poole writes, "Suddenly from just ahead came two single rifle shots; and then, an instant later, the long, sharp ugly rattle of a machine-gun, and the hiss and buzz of bullets over our heads. At once there was panic everywhere; and in the next ten seconds I grew so absorbed in my own career that I had no time to look around. In the rush I was carried off my feet; I threw up my arms and was borne with the mob through an open gateway into a court.... I looked back upon the street and saw it black with people lying on their faces. Bullets were flying thick and fast, and from all up and down the Nevsky I could hear the crash of shop windows as men dove through to get indoors" (Poole, *"The Dark People": Russia's Crisis* [New York: Macmillan, 1918], 6–7).

[44] "Real Russians: Vivid Sketches and Interviews of Village Life," *New York Tribune*, 16 November 1918, 9. "It is one of the most enlightening books on the Russian problem that have been written since the revolution."

York, but left immediately for Washington to deliver messages from Bullard to Creel at the Committee for Public Safety. The latter recruited Poole to head the New York office of a new Foreign Press Bureau, where he remained until the agency closed soon after the armistice.[45]

In the 1920s Poole returned to writing fiction, producing one novel a year for his faithful publisher, Macmillan, despite the fact that they were not as well received as his first two novels: *Blind* (1920),[46] *Beggars' Gold* (1921), *Millions* (1922), *Danger* (1923), *Avalanche* (1924), *Hunter's Moon* (1925), *With Eastern Eyes* (1926), and *Silent Storm* (1927). Russia was not forgotten—in *Avalanche* its influence can be seen in the narrator's recollection of Russian folk tales and in the apearance of characters possessing the power to cure afflictions through telepathy or hypnosis—but it had clearly receded from Poole's view.[47] Though Poole continued to produce fiction into the early 1930s, in particular works about the Depression, he became interested in depicting the real world, writing primarily at his summer home at Sugar Hill, near Franconia in the White Mountains.[48] Having lost much of his family inheritance in the stock market crash of 1929, he was now writing primarily out of necessity.

Poole's personal experience of financial calamity also revived his concern for the fate of the lower classes, on whom the Depression had inflicted the greatest suffering. Proving that the writing of his earlier settlement years was not mere muckraking for financial gain, he wrote letters to the editor of the *Times*, for example, about the plight of the "Bottom of the Bowery," the poorest of the Bowery's poor, who resorted to drinking cheap wood alcohol, "Smoke";[49] he ended his letter with a plea for donations to the Bowery YMCA and Salvation Army Hotel.[50]

This phase of Poole's career is perhaps more interesting to the historian, though his writing cites few sources, relying instead on the reporter's technique of weaving interview material into stories. His first book of nonfiction since *The Village* was

---

[45] Poole, *The Bridge*, 321–31; "Foreign Press Bureau Is Disbanded by Creel," *New York Tribune*, 20 December 1918, 5.

[46] "The Author of The Harbor Goes Adrift in His Latest Book: *Blind* is Overly Ambitious," *New York Tribune*, 24 October 1920, F9.

[47] Ernest Poole, *The Little Dark Man and Other Russian Sketches* (New York: Macmillan, 1925); Poole, "Mother Volga (as told me by a Russian friend)," *The Independent*, 20 December 1924, 537–38.

[48] Ernest Poole, *Great Winds* (New York: Macmillan, 1933); and Poole, *One of Us* (New York: Macmillan, 1934). Critics seem to agree that the latter, while not great, was much better than the former, which should not have been published (Keefer, *Ernest Poole*, 146–51).

[49] Ernest Poole, "'Smoke' on the Bowery," letter to the editor, *New York Times*, 7 February 1929, 21.

[50] Ernest Poole, "Unemployed Still Unemployed: Spring Has Not Come to the Bowery," letter to the editor, *New York Times*, 25 April 1931, 13.

*Nurses on Horseback* (1932), which drew inspiration from his settlement experience and admiration for Lillian Wald. This time the heroine was Mary Breckinridge, a woman from a distinguished Virginia family who became a midwife devoted to serving the poor in the mountains of eastern Kentucky and who founded the Frontier Nursing Service in May 1925. By 1932 the Service had grown to thirty-two nurses with over eight thousand patients. Poole himself traveled the region on horseback, accompanied by a nurse, to gather material.[51] The book was quite successful and became required reading at some nursing schools.[52]

Poole's next major work of nonfiction was his autobiography, *The Bridge* (1940). It was also published by Macmillan and included a number of photographs from his Russian and Caucasian tours of 1905 and 1917. The work emphasized Poole's childhood in Chicago and settlement years in New York, his experience as a reporter, his unsuccessful ventures into drama, and initial success as a novelist. Despite a disappointing dearth of information on Poole's family and the many individuals who were personal and professional associates, as well as its failure to discuss some of his more notable publications, *The Bridge* does provide an account of his travels and career. It attracted an audience that shared the author's nostalgia for the lost hopes of the early twentieth century and the American dream that a peaceful, progressive world would follow the horrors of the Great War and the Depression.[53] And the book provided valuable vignettes of people he knew, such as Woodrow Wilson, Mark Twain (from Greenwich Village), Maxim Gorky, Big Bill Haywood, Robert Frost (a neighbor in New Hampshire), William Dean Howells, O. Henry, and Lincoln Steffens. Poole was especially disappointed by the outcome of the Russian Revolution and, perhaps influenced by his recent visit to Italy, predicted the clash between dictatorships (particularly those led by Mussolini and Hitler) and the democratic countries that opposed them.[54]

Another big project undertaken by Poole, *Giants Gone: Men Who Made Chicago*, was likely motivated by the years spent listening to his father's stories of growing up in Chicago.[55] Poole traveled to Chicago to look up old friends and conduct interviews, though a number of sources were undocumented. As with the omissions that marred *The Bridge*, many of the founders of modern Chicago were left out or barely mentioned

---

[51] Keefer, *Ernest Poole*, 144–47.

[52] Ernest Poole, *Nurses on Horseback* (New York: Macmillan, 1932).

[53] Rose Feld, "Ernest Poole Reviews Six Decades of Personal History," *New York Times*, 25 August 1940, 74. See also Ralph Thompson, "Books of the Times," *New York Times*, 14 August 1940, 23.

[54] Keefer, *Ernest Poole*, 158–59.

[55] Ernest Poole, *Giants Gone: Men Who Made Chicago* (New York: Whittlesey House [McGraw-Hill], 1943).

and quite a bit of the corruption that was so characteristic of old Chicago was whitewashed. Still, the *New York Times* gave it a full-page review.[56]

Interestingly, while living in New York during the winter of 1942–43, Poole returned to the theme of *The Harbor* by visiting a New York waterfront bustling with troops and munitions bound for Europe, including a troop ship preparing to set sail. Naturally, he could not disclose details about its destination, but photographs accompanying his feature article graphically revealed the crowded quarters on board.[57]

Poole's final works reflected his love for New Hampshire, where he spent most of his later years. The first, *The Great White Hills of New Hampshire* is simply a tribute to the history and beauty of the state.[58] The second, *The Nancy Flyer: A Stagecoach Epic*, published in the last year of his life, is a fictional account of a real stagecoach of the Concord Coach line that Poole discovered in a New Hampshire barn. The book was, in fact, commissioned by his son William, who worked for a publisher (Thomas Y. Crowell).[59] This coach may well have reminded Poole of an episode described in *"The Dark People,"* when Tarasov showed Poole the ruins of an eighteenth-century French coach that had belonged to his grandmother and told the story that went with it.

After suffering two strokes, the second debilitating, Ernest Poole died in New York on January 10, 1950, just short of his seventieth birthday. An obituary stressed his role as a writer whose work portrayed the "other half" of New York City's population and as a reporter who rendered scenes and events subtly, yet graphically. A follow-up noted that he would be best remembered for *The Harbor* and *The Bridge*, concluding, "And until all his generation is gone he will be remembered as a warm and unselfish human being."[60] Poole's widow lived nearly another twenty years in the same New York apartment and at Sugar Hill, near Franconia in New Hampshire. She was survived by two sons, a daughter, and seven grandchildren.[61]

☙ ❧

Poole describes the Russian countryside of 1917 as a land transitioning from communal farming to individual ownership, from backwardness to modernity, portrayed in vivid descriptions of local characters: a new, educated priest; an eager and ambitious

---

[56] Frank S. Adams, "Chicago's Builders," *New York Times*, May 7, 1943, BR9.

[57] Poole, "The Port of a Thousand Secrets," *New York Times*, January 31, 1943, SM19, 33.

[58] *The Great White Hills of New Hampshire* (New York: Doubleday, Doran, 1946).

[59] *The Nancy Flyer: A Stagecoach Epic* (New York: Thomas Y. Crowell, 1949).

[60] "The Days of Ernest Poole," *New York Times*, January 13, 1950, 22. *See also* "Ernest Poole, 69, Novelest, is Dead," ibid., January 11, 1950, 20.

[61] "Mrs. Poole, 87, Dies: Widow of Novelist," *Chicago Tribune*, May 11, 1968, A14.

schoolteacher; a "prince" fading away in a derelict mansion; an enterprising farmer; and, finally, a young Finnish girl aspiring to be a doctor. This optimistic, progressive scene is contrasted with the revolutionary turmoil of the city, which is resented by the peasants and villagers, who provide labor, food, and soldiers but receive nothing in return.

The reader is left with a big question: what happened to all of that? Poole apparently did not follow up and had no further contact with this "real" Russia after 1917. His central character, hero, and "coauthor", Tarasov, seems to have disappeared, apparently consumed by the revolution. Was this the fate of this Russia?

## Suggested Additional Reading

Figes, Orlando. *A People's Tragedy: The Russian Revolution, 1891–1924.* New York: Penguin, 1998.

Heenan, Louise Erwin. *Russian Democracy's Fatal Blunder: The Summer Offensive of 1917.* New York: Praeger, 1987.

Jackson, George D., and Robert James Devlin, eds. *Dictionary of the Russian Revolution.* New York: Greenwood Press, 1989.

Keefer, Truman Frederick. *Ernest Poole.* New York: Twayne Publishers, 1966.

Lieven, D. C. B. *The End of Tsarist Russia: The March to World War I and Revolution.* New York: Viking, 2015.

Lincoln, W. Bruce. *Passage Through Armegeddon: The Russians in War and Revolution, 1914-1918.* New York: Oxford University Press, 1994.

Pares, Bernard. *Russia between Reform and Revolution: Fundamentals of Russian History and Character.* New York: Schocken Books, 1966.

Poole, Ernest. *The Bridge: My Own Story.* New York: The Macmillan Company, 1940.

———. *"The Dark People": Russia's Crisis.* New York: The Macmillan Company, 1918.

———. *Giants Gone: Men Who Made Chicago.* New York: Whittlesey House (McGraw-Hill), 1943.

———. *His Family.* New York: The Macmillan Company, 1917.

———. *The Harbor.* New York: The Macmillan Company, 1915.

———. *"The Little Dark Man" and Other Russian Sketches.* New York: The Macmillan Company, 1925.

Rabinowitch, Alexander. *The Bolsheviks Come to Power: The Revolution of 1917 in Petrograd.* New York: W. W. Norton, 1976.

———. *Prelude to Revolution: The Petrograd Bolsheviks and the July 1917 Uprising.* Bloomington: Indiana University Press, 1968.

Robinson, Geroid T. *Rural Russia Under the Old Regime.* London: Longmans, Green, 1932.

Rosenberg, William G. *Liberals in the Russian Revolution: The Constitutional Democratic Party, 1917–1921.* Princeton, NJ: Princeton University Press, 1974.

Saul, Norman E. *War and Revolution: The United States and Russia, 1914–1921.* Lawrence: University Press of Kansas, 2001.

Steinberg, Mark D. *The Russian Revolution, 1905–1921.* New York: Oxford University Press, 2016.

Stockdale, Melissa Kirschke. *Paul Miliukov and the Quest for a Liberal Russia, 1880–1918*. Ithaca, NY: Cornell University Press, 1996.

Wade, Rex A. *The Russian Revolution, 1917*. 3rd ed. Cambridge: Cambridge University Press, 2017.

# EDITORIAL NOTE

The text that follows is complete as originally published. Only a few alterations have been made. For example, to modernize it and to make it more readable some changes have been made—*rouble* has been converted to *ruble* and *Bolsheviki* to *Bolsheviks*, but the old form of *Czar* has been retained rather than *Tsar*. Also, transliterations of names and terms occur in current Library of Congress form: *desiatina* for *desatina*, for example. Explanatory material in the text is rendered as follows: parentheses ( ) are the author's; brackets [ ] the editor's. Footnotes provide additional annotated material. A few short paragraphs have also been joined. Anglicisms, such as *labour* for *labor*, were already removed from the text, in contrast to Poole's previous work, also published the year before by Macmillan.

# ACKNOWLEDGMENTS

About three years ago, Ben Whistenhunt and I began discussing a plan to republish books by Americans who witnessed the Russian Revolution of 1917, with the approaching centennial in mind. This series owes much to Ben, who has borne most of the communications with the people involved. We were also fortunate to find that the editors at Slavica Publishers, namely George Fowler and Vicki Polansky of Indiana University, supported our idea enthusiastically. We owe much to them and their assistants for exploring new territory in publishing on Russian history. At this moment, the first two books have been issued with several more on the way. Ben and I also appreciate the willingness of a number of scholars, both American and Russian, to join this project and devote their time and expertise in editing the individual volumes of the series.

# THE VILLAGE
## RUSSIAN IMPRESSIONS

By

Ernest Poole

Author of "The Harbor," "His Family," etc.

New York
THE MACMILLAN COMPANY
1919
[Published October, 1918]

To M. A.
[Margaret Ann, author's wife]

The author acknowledges the courtesy of the editors of *The New Republic* and *The Red Cross Magazine* in permitting the reprinting in this book of certain passages which first appeared in their magazines.

# Chapter I

## I

"Oh, Tarasov, hurry up!"

In my hotel room in Petrograd, Tarasov was doing his packing. I had already finished mine. It was a stifling afternoon in August, 1917, and we were trying to get off for a trip to a little village deep in the heart of the country. But I had small hope of catching the train. My companion was a man about forty, huge of limb and nearly bald. His face was flushed and perspiring. A vast, disorderly heap of belongings lay all around him on the floor, and he was mauling things about with a kind of desperate patience. To my imprecations he said not a word. I heard him panting softly.

In Petrograd and Moscow and in smaller cities, Juvenale Ivanovich Tarasov [Iuvenalii Ivanovich Tarasov] had for many weeks been my interpreter and friend. I had tried three other interpreters, two of them Bolsheviks and the third one a Cadet. Each had looked at Russia through his political party eyes. The value of Tarasov to me was that he belonged to no party at all. He belonged to Russia. He was a mixer. His view of his country had been formed through a career in which he had been a farmer, a chemical engineer, a high explosives expert and a maker of violins, a banker's clerk, a street traction man, a business promoter, a dreamer, an anthropologist for two years, a traveler, a great reader, and an eager translator of all kinds of foreign books. Years before in Russia, when I had first known him there, he had been translating Booker T. Washington's *Up From Slavery.* Then he had tackled another book and had come to me with a puzzled air, for he could not "get the eediom." It was *Mr. Dooley.*[1]

Tarasov was a fellow that one does not soon forget. I had kept in touch with him, and now on my second trip to Russia I searched until I found him at last, working in a Moscow bank. I telegraphed and he came at once. He arrived in Petrograd on the third night of the July Insurrection, when the Bolshevik Red Guards and the troops who supported Kerensky were fighting busily in the streets. Several hundred had been killed. You could still hear shots occasionally. I had been out and returned to my room about ten o'clock. Tarasov was waiting for me there. At my entrance he sprang up and gave me a long Russian embrace, with tears of real joy in his eyes. Then I drew back and surveyed him.

---

[1] Poole had met Tarasov when he was reporting on the 1905 revolution in Russia.

"What has happened to you?" I asked. He was haggard and pale. Plainly the revolution, I thought, had played the devil with my friend. As I looked at him, there came to our ears the rattle of shots from the Square of the Winter Palace close by. But Tarasov was thinking of other things.

"When she left me last week," he replied, "for fifty-two hours I lay on the floor like a man who is dead."

Then he told me in detail of this last love affair of his. What a beauty! What dark regular features, and a form that would have driven the old Greek sculptors to despair. In short, a goddess! He grasped my arm and walked me about in Petrograd until two o'clock in the morning. At times I would pitilessly interrupt and would make him converse for me with the groups of Kerensky soldiers and Red Guards who, upon street corners and out on the great bridges that spanned the misty Neva under the light of a yellow half moon, were still engaged in a little affair called "the Russian Revolution." But then my companion would return to the great topic on his mind. How he had labored with that girl, to educate her, give her a soul. They had lived together for two years; he had begged her to marry him, time and again. But she would not. And now—gone! He described his comatose condition after her departure. He intended to write it all down for the benefit of psychiatrists. On and on and on we walked. In short, a goddess! Well, she was gone. And what did he care for the girl, after all? There had been many others and there would be more! Meanwhile what a time we would have! He would show me all Russia—the whole revolution!

"You'll leave the bank?"

"Of course! Why not? What is a bank?" he joyously asked.

So our travels began. Six weeks passed; and now we were about to start on the very best of our journeys. For well as Tarasov knew the towns, he knew the villages better still. He himself was a small landowner, and today we were off to his estate, about five hours from Petrograd. In the morning he had left me to go to his mother's apartment here, to get some things we would need in the country.

"In an hour I shall return to you, my dear," he had assured me.

That was about six hours ago, for on the street he had met a friend and they had had one of those long Russian talks, wandering here and there over the town. In their wanderings, he had remembered to do as I had asked him—he had inquired about the trains. He had found there were three; and Tarasov was planning to catch the last, which left town at seven that night and arrived at a lonely junction somewhere off in the forest a bit after 3 a.m. At that hour, if we could find a rig, we would drive some thirty versts (twenty miles) to his estate. This was his program. I looked at him grimly.

"Tarasov," I said, "we have lost the first train because while you wandered off into the future of Russia with that bosom friend of yours, I was sitting sweating here! We will now catch the *second* train! Come on now—get busy! Pack!"

He grew very gloomy then, for this meant haste, which he despised. He looked at me in a puzzled way, as though he were trying to understand this weird Yankee

# CHAPTER I

love of speed. What earthly difference did it make whether we ended our journey in the dusk or in the dawn? But he patiently bent to his packing, while I quickly finished mine.

I was in a fever to get off. I was tired, my nerves on edge. I had had enough of the cities, with their endless arguing, their shouting crowds and street parades, packed meeting halls and stifling rooms, words and theories, heated quarrels over plans as dry as dust. I had felt about me the germs of something wonderful here, something deep, stupendous, real—warm as the very blood of life. But I had felt it being chilled and ossified by dogma. I had seen the revolution breaking into factions, with strikes and open rioting, machine guns spraying bullets up and down the dirty streets. And then what had happened? Just more talk! I was tired of their politics. I wanted to get beneath all that, down into the mass of the people themselves, to find again what had been lost—the great heart of the real revolution. And where were the Russian people? Nine-tenths of them were peasants in lonely little villages. I wanted to sink into their life.

Since the war began, I had lived in New York, with trips to London and Berlin, and out along the western front.[2] I was sick of the cities, one and all, with their shrill hates and jealousies, their war scandals and intrigues. Again and again there had come to me a feeling of the presence all around me, far and near, of the millions of villages in the world where the silent mass of the plain people dwell. I had done my traveling mostly by night, and often from a crowded train where travelers on every hand were arguing about the war, I had looked out on some little hamlet buried in a forest or nestling on a mountain-side, and seeing a light still burning in a dwelling here and there, I had longed to go into those huts and ask,

"What has the war done to you? How do you feel about all this?"

My eyes ached from the red glare of the Present. I wanted to live for awhile in a place where life ran deep, and was quiet enough so that one could feel the Present not by itself but as a gap, or a bridge, between the Past and Future.

Also, I wanted a little real food. The restaurants of Petrograd had held more noise than nourishment. I had grown lean, and I looked forward to this country journey of ours as to a camping trip back at home. But could I get Tarasov into the spirit of my plan? I could not. When I gave him my purse and asked him to go and stock up with what groceries we might need, his only answer was a smile.

"All that we require," he said, "we shall find at my estate."

"But you told me you had rented your place."

"It is true," he replied. "An old Finn is there with two Finnish servants."

"Better send them a wire that we are coming." Tarasov looked at me puzzled: "Why?"

---

[2] The author had reported early in 1915 on World War I for the *Saturday Evening Post*—from the German side.

"Because there may not be room enough!"

"There will be sufficient," he replied.

"But will they want us?"

"Probably."

"Suppose they have visitors of their own?"

"But they may not have any visitors."

I gave up in despair. It was hopeless to try to arouse in this man the least interest in my comfort. For he was no more practical than was the big nation to which he belonged—no more practical than its warfare, with the great Brusilov drives far down into Hungary,[3] and the chaotic vast retreats; no more practical than its revolution, seething with dreams when it should have been acting. Juvenale Ivanovich Tarasov[4] was an impractical man.

On that hot day in Petrograd, as he knelt perspiring on the floor, his eyes fairly bulged with his efforts, but nothing seemed to happen at all. He had lugged along from his mother's flat four heavy blankets and one sheet and two enormous pillows. There were also shirts and collars, a revolver and a suit of clothes, a hair brush and a cake of soap, two towels and a big pair of boots, a safety razor, many books, a tooth brush and a mowing scythe. He had taken the blade of the scythe from the handle and bound the two parts together with twine but even so it was hard to fit it in with the rest of his toilet set. All these things again and again he had feverishly pyramided on the blankets spread over the floor, and had tried to draw up the corners into one gigantic bag. So far, so good. But the moment he tried to hoist the bag, his things began to dribble out.

Impatiently I came to his aid. I am not much of a packer myself, but with the help of some good stout twine we soon made up a parcel about the size of a small stack of hay. I had rung for a porter, but none came; for the hotel porters had gone to attend a political meeting that afternoon. So we hurried downstairs with my suitcase, my sleeping bag and Tarasov's enormous immigrant bundle. We dumped them into a cab and were off.

Of that clattering drive down the Nevsky, I have only a vague memory now. I had seen it all so often—the same broad dusty thoroughfare with the crowded trolley cars, the countless little open cabs and peasants' carts and rumbling trucks, the troops of mounted Cossacks, the endless throngs of people on foot, Russians, Tartars, Gypsies, Georgians; the crowds in front of bulletin boards, the speeches on street corners.

---

[3] Reference is to the Galician offensive of April 1916 led by General Aleksei Alekseevich Brusilov (1853–1926). This was initially the most successful Russian military action of the war and inspired a similar initiative in 1917, the Kerensky offensive, which was a disaster.

[4] Iuvenalii is listed as a Russian male name though not very common. Iuvenalii Ivanovich Tarasov is pronounced with the accents on nal, van, and ras. Morton Benson, comp., *Dictionary of Russian Personal Names, With a Guide to Stress and Morphology* (Philadelphia: University of Pennsylvania Press, 2nd ed., 1969), 122, 170.

# CHAPTER I

Tarasov leaned back and mopped his brow, and then lit a cigarette. Our horse was galloping at the time and the cab was swaying to and fro, but Tarasov knew how to get a light in any place or weather. When we had slept in the same room, the tiny glow of his small weed would be the last light in the darkness; and, as he slept very heavily, in the morning as a rule I would entice him back to life by placing a cigarette in his mouth and lighting it. He would awake with a smile. He smiled now as he puffed, and surveyed with contempt a crowd gathered around a street-speaker.

"How they talk and talk and do nothing," he said.

He himself had concocted a plan to save the entire revolution. He had promised to show it to me in detail as soon as we reached his village. He started to speak of it now—as he always did on every occasion.

"I was explaining my plan in full to the friend I met today," he said. "I found him very sympathetique."

"I'll bet you did," I muttered grimly. I was thinking of our train. But Juvenale Ivanovich had his mind on higher things.

"If these confounded idiots would only remember," he began, "that nine-tenths of the Russians live in villages—and that until the question of land—"

"Stop the cab!" I suddenly cried. "You've forgotten those kodak films."

With a startled "Ah," Tarasov jumped out and followed me into a kodak shop. On the day before, they had had no films, but the shop-man had sworn he would have them today. He smiled at me now and began to explain how on account of the Great Revolution—which was going to such extremes that as for himself he was forced to believe *that* the only salvation for Russia —

"Come on, Tarasov! Can't you see he has no films?"[5]

"Yes, but I want to get his views."

"Oh, damn his views."

Juvenale Ivanovich followed me peevishly back to the cab.

"That's a fault of you Americans, and a devilish big one, too," he declared, as we galloped down the street "Speed, speed—you must have speed! And that fault in you may spoil the whole world! For if in impatience you give us up, Germany will step into your shoes and force herself on us as our friend. And that will make the world a hell! And all because you are crazy for speed and will not take time to understand. Here is a man belonging to the petit bourgeoisie and he offers to explain his views. But you for the mere sake of catching one damn train instead of another—"

"Here we are," I interrupted. We had arrived at the station twenty-five minutes ahead of time; but at first it seemed, as I had feared, that even so we had come too late—for at the ticket window was a line of a hundred or more, and by sad experience I knew that now at any moment the ticket seller might make up his mind that the train

---

[5] This may explain why no photographs are included in the book, though several are printed in *The Dark People*, which preceded this book.

was packed to bursting. Then he would slam his window down and we should all have a three-hour wait.

"I am afraid we have come too late," said Juvenale Ivanovich. Feverishly I grasped his arm.

"Tarasov," I ordered, "go to that chap near the head of the line and ask him to buy our tickets with his." I do not propose such things as a rule, but three hours more in Petrograd would have driven me half insane. Tarasov chuckled.

"Graft," he said. "American graft." He was proud of his Yankee "eedioms."

We got the tickets just before the little window was slammed down, and shouldering our luggage we hurried through the gate to our train.

The train was certainly crowded. It fairly bulged with people and things, especially bags and babies. The narrow platforms overflowed. But using his huge bundle like an impending load of hay, Tarasov forced a breach for us, and we clambered up on board just as the train began to move. Two fat little Chinamen were there. Tarasov lifted them firmly while I shoved our bags beneath. The Chinamen were placed on top, both of them smiling at the joke, and presently they fell asleep. The small platform was crowded to an ominous degree, with people clinging on the steps; but between the two cars was a swaying sheet of steel about a foot in width. On this we stepped and balanced ourselves by a grip upon the railing.

Creaking and groaning, the train made its way through yards that were crowded with freight cars which no one as yet had found time to unload. Locomotives stood about, with bell shaped smoke-stacks like the ones we used to have in America. Most of these Russian engines still burned little logs instead of coal, and now the sweet pungent smoke of wood came back to us on the hot wind. As we reached the suburbs our speed increased, until we were rocking and screeching along at nearly thirty miles an hour.

But this did not in the least prevent Juvenale Ivanovich, as he balanced on our sheet of steel, from conversing hungrily with his fellow travelers. These Russians are surely a sociable lot. Soon we were having a regular meeting out on those two narrow platforms, with jokes and laughter, scowls, discussions and tense earnest arguments. Only the two little Chinamen slept serenely, undisturbed. We were on the Trans-Siberian route, and their placid faces seemed to say, "Wake us up when we get to China." No doubt they felt that their country's time for all this sort of talk was still far off. But was it? I asked. I was not sure.

The Russians meanwhile were telling each other how the train service all over the country was now rapidly breaking down. Nobody seemed dismayed at the prospect. With keen animation they discussed how it would be to live without trains; and a large genial merchant claimed that it would be "an excellent thing for us all." Then we passed a forest where the underbrush was burning, filling the air with so much smoke that it was difficult to breathe. But did that stop us? Not at all. It merely led to a most absorbing talk on the forest problem. The peasants were jealous, somebody said, of having any trees cut down, for they felt that the forests were soon to be theirs. So the supply of wood was low, and there would be undoubtedly a famine of fuel in the cities during the long cold winter ahead. After that, they talked of the war. This, too, was going badly. Only one young ensign, plainly a born optimist, had anything good to say of the army. But when he described the improvement of morale on his sector of the front, a lean cadaverous captain squelched him with the gloomy remark that now not only the army but the entire nation, too, was riding for a heavy fall. After that, a student girl asked me what we thought of them over in America. And from the many questions thrown at me from every side, I got the same impression I had so often had before, of the eagerness in Russia to learn about American life. There are some Russians who despise us, more who smilingly criticize, but the great mass of these people simply want to be our friends.

More and more travelers left the train. Tarasov and his "sympathetiques" adjourned to seats inside the car, and I was left on the platform alone with the two Chinamen. The heat of the day was over; the rush of air was cooler now. The stations were smaller and farther apart. Some were mere log cabins with stretches of forest on either hand. The dusk deepened. I breathed hungrily the fresh piney air that came out of the woods. Sitting on a step of the car, I watched the shadowy trees whirl by, and the occasional clearings, with lights shining out of windows in lonely little huts of logs. It was good to be in the country.

When we reached our destination, instantly there was a rush of people to get on our train. There seemed to be hundreds, for this was a junction. How they shouted, clutched and shoved! But we managed to jerk our bags from under the two Chinamen, and with our belongings made our way into the station restaurant, a large, dirty, crowded room with a counter running along one side. At the two long tables, the clatter and talk made a deafening noise. All kinds of travelers were here—officers, soldiers, sailors, civilians, rough simple peasants and city folk, agitators from Petrograd, sober merchants from small towns, rich and poor and young and old, swarms of children, babies crying. Here were whole families moving; here were all sorts and conditions of people, jarred loose from their moorings in the storm, meeting in this eddy and seizing the chance to talk it all over. The Great Revolution!

We drank our tea and hungrily devoured boiled potatoes, greasy meatballs, and big fresh cucumbers. While we ate, Tarasov questioned the waiter, who discussed in a cheerful way how everything in this neighborhood was rapidly going from bad to worse. The price for a conveyance to take us to my friend's estate had risen to twenty-five rubles—about three times the former amount. Moreover, the waiter doubted if there was a hack or a cart to be hired at this time of night. I looked reproachfully at my friend, who finished his supper and hurried out. He returned and reported no success.

"Never mind," he said, "I have with a little money persuaded a soldier fellow—and he will help us carry our bags to a steamboat on the river. It is about two miles from here. We shall pass the night on board, and early tomorrow the boat will take us immediately to my estate. My place is on the river bank. We shall leap from the steamer as it goes by."

With a young husk of a soldier tramping ahead with most of our luggage, we started up along the track. We passed first through the train yard amid a perfect bedlam of hoots and piercing shrieks from engines. Headlights glared from every side. Then we came out on the long dark road, and the noise died down behind us. It was a bleak, flat country, with little woods and fields and marshes. Above us, on the high embankment, bare-footed country people passed—mere silent shadows. Out of the darkness just ahead, an old peasant emerged abruptly, leading a bony little horse. With a whispered imprecation, our soldier lad threw down his burden. The night air was warm and humid here, and we stood resting for a while. More silent figures flitted by. A frog was croaking in the marsh. With a sigh, the soldier heaved his load up onto his back, and on we trudged.

At last we came to the river. Overhead, the great long railroad bridge was dark except for some little red lights; but underneath it was brilliantly lighted by the glare of search-lights—there were two at either end. I could see armed guards down there—and above on the track, by the little red lights, the small dark shadow of a soldier pacing slowly to and fro. Our road turned to the left on the high river bank, then pitched abruptly down the slope and brought us to the landing. Here lay a small river steamer. She was absolutely dark, but from somewhere within her, we heard a murmur of voices. We struck matches, climbed the gangplank and came into a long low stuffy cabin. We searched till we found a candle there, and with this we explored a bit. We could still hear the rough murmur of voices, and my indefatigable friend scented a "meeting" of some kind. Near the stern we found a steel ladder, and descending we came down into a stifling little place where a group of boatmen—four of them big bearded creatures, and three hardly more than boys—were intent on a game of cards, each one with his pile of paper money in front of him. They glanced up at our intrusion, then went hungrily on with the game. One of the youngsters gave a low laugh and swept in a few more rubles. At this a huge chap with a short black beard glared suddenly up; his eye caught mine, and he stared at me in gloomy reproach, as though blaming me for his losses. Tarasov found no "meeting" here. In answer to his questions, they told us curtly that the boat would start at six in the morning, and that we could sleep where we liked.

We climbed up again to the cabin. Along either side ran a narrow seat of dirty red velvet. Loud snoring could be heard at one end. Tarasov began to prepare for the night, but I did not like this stuffiness, so I took my sleeping bag and went out on the upper deck. Here the air was cool and fresh. The night was still. Above me, little wreaths of smoke floated out of the steamer's funnel. I lay down on the deck and for some time looked drowsily up at the distant stars. Now and then a dog barked in the distance, and I could hear the tinkle of cow-bells from across the river. Presently a row-boat passed, and I heard a low voice talking. Then from down the river there

# CHAPTER I

came to my ears a tenor voice singing a plaintive melody, in a rhythm which made me feel that the singer was rowing—his head thrown back.

Just a short way down the river loomed the great heavy span of the bridge. Every few minutes a train came by. With the shriek of its engine echoing with a weird effect against the limestone quarries cut into the high river banks, the train would thunder across the bridge, leaving behind a long white tail of wood smoke rising slowly into the dark vault of the sky. Nearly all the trains from Petrograd, that were bound for the Trans-Siberian journey, passed this way. I thought of the crowds in those hot cars, arguing, arguing, arguing; and I thanked God I was out of it all—the fever and the endless talk, the mere froth and surface storm. Now and then I could hear the splash of a fish. It was good to be in the country.

I thought of the numberless spots like this, upon which these same silent stars were throwing their mysterious light—dark rivers running still and deep, rock-bound coasts along the sea, forests, mountains, valleys, plains; and of the countless villages all over this war-ridden world. Into each the war had come, and had worked such changes through the years that life would never again be the same. I thought of a village dear to me in the mountains of New Hampshire. I had been there three months before. War had just begun to affect it then. Five of its boys had been drafted, and their parents were buying maps of Europe and the danger zones. Now every day and every night their thoughts and fancies would be led out over the seas to villages with foreign names, some horribly torn and blackened by war, others with the buildings standing but with the souls of the dwellers changed. These villages all over the world, would they come to know each other any better after the war? Only in such understanding lay any hope of a lasting peace.

## 2

I fell asleep, and a few hours later I was awakened by voices. They seemed to come from far below. I felt daylight and a fresh damp mist upon my face, but I did not open my eyes. Dog tired from the night before, I lay half dozing, drifting there, high up in the mist and the light of the dawn. Higher and higher, lighter, lighter—now I was soaring in the clouds, now bathed in the radiance of the sun. But the earth below me was as dark and dim as a dream. It was like a great ghostly encampment made up of numberless villages. The one in New Hampshire was dose by, nestling on its mountain-side. Farther down was a village in France with tall poplars in long rows. There were some Russian hamlets, too. These were all I could make out; the others were mere shadowy blurs. Off they scattered over the earth. Why so dark? Suddenly I opened my eyes, for with a sharp twinge I remembered the war.

The boat was enveloped in cool white mist, through which I could see the dear blue of the dawn. Now the voices were close beside me. Travelers coming on the boat. I remembered that the last train from the city was due to arrive at about this time. These people had doubtless come on the train which Tarasov would have taken. All my haste had been for this. I smiled grimly at myself. Nevertheless, I argued, this was a heap sight better than sitting up all night in a car. The travelers as they came on board did not seem in the least surprised to find a man in a sleeping bag. They took me quite as a matter of course, a part of the Great Revolution, perhaps. And I was very grateful for that. What decent chaps these Russians were! They had gone to another part of the deck and left me to finish my night's sleep.

Later I was aroused again by the coming of more travelers. This time I rolled up my bag and went ashore for a little walk. The river bank had awakened to life. On the barges moored around our boat, the women were cooking breakfast, while all along the waterside the men were harnessing their teams of runty little mules and horses. Long sagging ropes were stretched from the shore. There were so many barges, it seemed a hopeless tangle. There were shouts and the cracking of whips. Six small horses in single file would begin to strain on their harness and move slowly up the tow-path, while behind a barge would emerge from the others and start sluggishly up the stream.

Ravenously hungry now, I went back on our boat and down into the cabin. I found it filled with people sitting at small tables. A cabin boy was serving tea. Tarasov was chatting with a group of three old friends he had discovered. They brought out from their bags hard boiled eggs and chunks of black bread which they shared with us, and so we made our breakfast. These friends, Tarasov explained to me, were small landowners like himself, living in his neighborhood. One was a country doctor. All of them were of peasant birth.

"You must get their point of view," he said. "You must not think of our peasants as an ignorant hopeless mass. It is not so. With real education they will build a very wonderful nation here. The proof of this is that even under the Old Régime, which treated the peasants like so many dogs, strong men kept rising out of them. Some went to the cities and got rich. In Moscow are many millionaires who began life in peasant huts. And in the villages themselves are the men who are shrewd and thrifty—like these three who are sitting here. Though few in numbers, they are the natural strong men of their neighborhoods, and they are bound to make themselves heard. As the revolution goes on, I think that all our Russian life will fall into such a devil's mess that the peasants will turn to these practical chaps. Then you will see what we shall do!"

Meanwhile the country doctor had a newspaper in his hands, and was reading to the others the latest news from Petrograd. The doctor was a spare little man with thin sandy hair, a snub nose, square jaws, and small black eyes that twinkled and snapped through his spectacles. As he read in a quick incisive voice, the others

# CHAPTER I

listened intently. One was a man about fifty years old, short, thick-set, with hulking shoulders and large freckled bony hands, a heavy bearded face, blue eyes.

"A fine government this is," he growled, "getting ready to rob us of our land. Tovarisch (comrade)—how tired I am of that word. Now any thief is my tovarisch. Last week to our district court a fellow was brought for stealing a horse; and he was in rags, the devil. He smiled at the judge and called him 'tovarisch.' But the judge gave it to him right. 'I am not your tovarisch,' he said. 'You are a thief and I am a judge!' But the fellow in rags only laughed at him and said, 'Then you are a lonely man.' And he was right, the scoundrel! A judge or any other man with any sense or honesty is lonely enough in Russia, these days especially in the government. What are they but a pack of thieves? 'Save the revolution!' they cry. But no one says, 'Save Russia!' And what they really mean by it all is that they want to save themselves. Now to prolong their revolution, they will start a civil war. Their new land committee here is surveying all the land, getting ready to divide it up. But if they try this devil's scheme they will split Russia wide apart—for we will fight before we give in!" The landowner banged his huge fist on the table. "Slowly, slowly, year by year for generations, ever since the Emancipation when we were no longer serfs, for the land we received we have paid and paid in taxes to the government. And now I say we will never give up! These socialists talk of the bourgeois. I tell you that the peasant is the first bourgeois in the land! He will not give up what he has! Like iron he will close his fists!"

Then the other, a tall stooping man with black hair and a lean unshaven face, put down his glass of tea and said, in a slow impassive tone:

"I have worked on my land for thirty-one years. I have cleared it of shrubs and saplings. I have plowed up fifty desiatinas (125 acres) of soil and have watered every rod with my sweat. I dug out the stumps by the hundred. The land was all roots, but I plowed and plowed, and then I harrowed and harrowed again. Will I let them take it from me now? They may kill me first." He stopped with a frown. And his big companion continued:

"These Bolsheviks are as shrewd a lot as you could find. They want to divide all property here—but they themselves have taken good care to sell out what they own and invest every ruble in Germany. In Russia a dozen pawn tickets are their sole belongings. What do they care for Russia? All they do is against the war! Here in our district, a tract of forest was to have been cut for the needs of the army—and that was right. But along came a Jew from Petrograd to tell the peasants not to allow it. 'These forests are now all yours,' he said, 'and you must not allow the trees to be cut!' I owned some of those trees myself, and I had sold them at a good price—and here these devils stopped the sale! I tell you they are all alike! Our only hope is in Mother Moscow, where the people have some sense. They should cut the rails to Petrograd and let that city starve to death. Their government is no government. Did we elect these Feinbergs, these Applebaums and Rosenzweigs? Are they *our* chosen people? Oh, no, my friends! They chose themselves!"

"Why don't you copy them? Choose yourself," said the little doctor, drily. "All you need is a piece of board. Paint on it, 'Russian Government.' Then take it to Petrograd, rent an office, hang the board outside the door." But the big man snorted angrily.

"They will not get a single grain of wheat or rye from our villages until they stop their tricks!" he cried. "They won't make us open our granaries by promising their money, the thieves, for their rubles are worth nothing at all.[6] And how they have wrecked the army, too! The shame of the Tarnopol retreat could have been avoided, if they had not months before stopped the death penalty at the Front. It should be restored both at the Front and in the Rear! But will they do it? Not at all! Because these fellows know too well that they themselves would be the very first candidates for the gallows! But when every peasant sees their game, then they will dance between heaven and earth. Thank God, the Cossacks will soon take charge, and then in our district we'll use that old gallows up on the hill. A man swinging there could be seen from far off, and it would be good for the scenery!"

The big man stopped. He was breathing hard.

There was a short pause, and then the country doctor said, softly but with an ominous smile:

"These tovarischi speak of an eight-hour day. They call me a bourgeois loafer. 'Let the masses work only eight hours,' they say, 'and put this idle chap to work.' Very well, brothers, let's see about that. I have worked for the Zemstvo (the district legislature) for something over twenty years, from six in the morning till twelve at night. I have gone to the sick all over the country, summer and winter. I have worn out three sledges, and God knows how many horses, too. I could not tell how many hundreds of nights I have spent in driving around, with no sleep to speak of for nearly a week. And out of my earnings, bit by bit, I bought ninety desiatinas of land—and by hard work and planning I put the woodland in good shape and the rest under cultivation. So now I'm a bourgeois loafer, eh? Did I not honestly serve the State—both in curing thousands of patients and in cultivating the land? But they call me a bourgeois, and my land must be taken away! Suppose that it happened? What would it do? It would level down my standards to those of the lowest peasants here. All that I have done would be lost! And Russia cannot risk such waste! We must not sink down into the mass; we must force it slowly up—go after the peasants and make them stop living in filth and every kind of disease; go after the land and plow it up and teach the peasants how to farm!"

This was the cue for Tarasov to broach to them his own pet plan for the salvation of Russia. Soon he was talking eagerly. But I had heard enough for the present. I left the stuffy cabin and went up for a breath of fresh air.

---

[6] A major problem for the Russian government in 1917 was runaway inflation. Added to this situation by 1917 was a dearth of manufactured goods available in the countryside, because of the shifting of priorities to war production and the reduced output due to shortages of fuel and raw materials.

# CHAPTER I

The deck of the steamer was crowded now, but I found a seat up in the bow, where the fresh delicious breeze was sweet with the smell of the hay and the pines. The wide river ran smoothly between high banks, in a flat country with fields on each side, and woods and rolling meadows. Every mile or so was a hamlet, a straggling row of log huts and barns, and then would come a larger village, where we would stop at a primitive wharf. The banks of the river were lined with logs that had come from the forests of the North and were bound for Petrograd. They had been brought down the stream in rafts to a cataract above us, where the rafts had been broken up and the logs had come tumbling down, to be reassembled here and so continue their journey to the distant capital. We passed several great unwieldy rafts. On each a group of men and boys guided it with sweeps and poles. One such group was singing. We met many peasant fishermen, in dories and queer little canoes. When we stopped, some of them came alongside, and we bought two fish for our dinner.

Tarasov, who had come on deck, said that we were near his home. He spoke to the captain, who promptly blew two piercing blasts, and after that, as the boat slowed down, from a cluster of fishing dories ahead, one was rowed rapidly toward us. We hastened below with our luggage; and from the open gangway there, as the dory came alongside, we threw in our bags and jumped after them. At once the steamer went ahead, and we were left in the dory with a gray old peasant. He rowed us to the high wooded bank. We paid him a ruble, went ashore across a raft of huge brown logs, and climbed a steep and winding path through a grove of white birches, maples, and firs. We passed an old well with a bucket and came to a large log cabin above. And here Juvenale Ivanovich drew a quiet breath and said:

"This is the place where I was born."

## 3

The cabin stood on a wooded bluff. Behind was a small barnyard with a row of barns and stables, little huddling log affairs. To one side was a hut, which Tarasov leased for a nominal rent to a peasant who worked the land with him on shares. On the other side was a ravine, and across it I could see through the trees a yellow frame house, which belonged to a certain Prince C—.

"Now you see my position," Tarasov said. "I am between the prince and the peasant. My father was a peasant's son; my mother was of noble birth. And if you would get any real idea of our Russian life in its deeper part, you must not forget the hundreds of thousands of small landowners like myself, scattered all over the country."

We entered the cabin with our bags, and came first into the kitchen, a roomy place with brown log walls. Heavy beams ran overhead, and one corner was wholly filled by an enormous old brick stove with a massive chimney. The stout Finnish woman there seemed to know Tarasov, but her greeting was not cordial. With a grim worried look in her eyes, she motioned to us to talk low. Her master was very sick, she said, and she had sent her daughter to fetch the doctor from the town, which was some nine miles away. Cautiously she opened the door of a room where her master lay asleep. A heavy old man of nearly eighty, his face was gray; he looked very weak. And when the woman had closed the door, I suggested that we go away. But Tarasov saw no reason. There was plenty of room, he said; and besides, we should be here only to sleep.

From the kitchen we had come into a small living room. On one side was a glass-enclosed porch, and at the end was the studio of Tarasov's father, who had been a painter. It was a square room with walls of logs. To the left were three big windows, and to the right a great stove of tile which extended up to the ceiling and was painted gray and blue. There was a window at the end, with a drafting board before it, and a large wooden easel nearby with an unfinished canvas. Others stood against the walls. There was a tall chest of drawers in one corner, and a narrow mahogany bed. But what a curious bedroom! For all his life Tarasov had had a passion for farming, and he had lived with his hobby here. A mud encrusted American plow leaned against the foot of the bed, and a harrow lay on the floor close by. Near it were a crowbar and a shovel and two spades. Beside the three large windows ran a wooden work-bench littered with tools of every kind. Other tools hung on the walls, and there were skiis and snow-shoes and a rifle hanging there. Close by stood a grindstone. I stumbled over a rake on the floor.

"Tarasov," I said earnestly, "I hope you do not walk in your sleep."

"This will be your bedroom," said my host. I looked a bit dubious, and he asked: "Or would you prefer the room upstairs?"

"Let's see it," I suggested, and he took me back to the kitchen, from which by a steep stairway we climbed to a long dark attic above. On one side was a little room with two dormer windows that looked through the trees down to the murmuring river below. Here I brought my baggage and then rejoined Tarasov outdoors.

Juvenale Ivanovich was very happy to be home. With a quiet affectionate pride he showed me the barn and the stable, the granary and the wood-shed—four little log buildings in a row. He showed me farming implements that he himself had made as a boy, and he spoke of the time when living here he had run a dairy farm, with sixteen cows. Now they were gone. Near the house lay a big dory, with iron sheathing on the sides to protect it from the river ice when he had fished in the early spring. This, he told me, he had built when he was a youngster of eighteen. He lifted the bow about a foot—a fairly creditable feat, for it must have weighed three hundred pounds. But he seemed suddenly much depressed.

# CHAPTER I

"I am not so strong as I was. I am getting old," he grimly remarked. "Three years ago when I was here I could carry that boat on my back all the way down to the river." He sighed regretfully. "In those days I was in fine trim. I shall tell you why. The year before that, I had not felt well; and so, all at once in a single day, I stopped smoking and drinking, I stopped eating meat, I gave up even eggs or milk. For an entire year, my friend, I lived on bread and vegetables. The result was like a miracle! The strength of my youth had come again!"

He went on to explain in detail the wonders of vegetarian diet. But I was a poor listener. In the kitchen my hungry eye had roved about for signs of provisions, with discouraging results.

"Speaking of food," I suggested, "I'm not at all sure that with a sick man in the house this woman will want us here for meals."

"Oh," said Tarasov vaguely, "we shall have no trouble here." And he banished the whole thought of food with one careless wave of the hand. I looked at him bitterly. What a host!

"Now we shall have a swim!" he announced. To this I readily agreed. We took soap and towels and went down to the river, and from the big raft of logs we slipped into the dark soft water. For a time we washed and swam about. Later, when we had climbed the bluff, we visited the hut next door where the peasant lived who worked the farm; and there in the low kitchen a small neat-looking woman, with a strong but tired face, served us with a loaf of bread and a big earthen jar of milk. While she eagerly talked with Tarasov, I kept watching curiously; for to me she seemed more German than Slav. And in this I found that I was right.

"She was born and raised," my friend explained, "in one of the Baltic provinces, where there has been a considerable mixing of Russian and of Teuton blood. As for this woman, I like her—but as a sign of the times she is bad. For these Germans little by little are spreading all through Russia. There are probably several millions now, scattered about in the provinces. They intermarry and settle down. Here comes her husband," he added. "You will see that he is pure Russian."

The husband was a tall lumbering man, with a full, heavy, ruddy face and a thick brown beard that was flecked with gray. He had been plowing out on the field, and obviously he was delighted at this excuse for stopping work. His face was one enormous smile and his small eyes had a genial gleam, as he held out his hand to Tarasov and cried in a deep ringing bass:

"Zdrastvitch, Juvenale Ivanovich! Zdrastvitch!" Which in English means, "Good health to you!" He lit a little cigarette and settled down for a long Russian talk.

The new plow that Tarasov had sent him, he said, was now working splendidly. True, he had been able to plow only half as much ground as Tarasov had hoped; but this, he explained with his genial smile, was due to the fact that he had only one little horse on the farm. The other horses had been taken long ago for the army. As to the war, he had nothing to say. Plainly he was indifferent. For the horse that was left, which he owned himself, he had paid forty rubles some years ago. "Now I am offered four hundred," he said, "but I will not sell him. For money is good for nothing, these days. I can't hitch rubles to the plow—so I keep my horse and do my best." Then he broke the cheerful news that he had sold all but two of the cows. There was little or no manure, and he wanted Tarasov to buy him a ton or so of fertilizer. We soon grew tired of his talk.

"I have no use for that chap," said my friend, after we had left the hut. "He is always asking for something new—something I must buy at once or the farm will go to rack and ruin. He does nothing but talk, talk, all day and let his wife and daughters work. Look, how he keeps his barnyard!"

It was a stinking wallow of filth. Farming implements lay in the mud. By the pigsty two slim girls, about twelve and fourteen years of age, in dirty cotton dresses, were feeding slops and garbage to an old yellow sow and her litter.

"Their father won't let them go to school," said Juvenale Ivanovich.

"Why don't you get rid of the man?" I demanded impatiently. "This is a bad beginning, my friend, of that practical plan you were going to show me."

"Oh, this is nothing," he replied. "I have only eight desiatinas (about twenty acres) here. It is on my larger farm, two miles away, that I am working out my experiment and there I have as a partner quite a different kind of chap. You must not be discouraged if I show you the very worst of our peasants first. Now we shall see something better."

We went to another little farm about five minutes' walk down the river. This place had a more thrifty air. In fact, there was painful evidence on every side of constant toil. The clothes of the three small children had been patched and patched again; the hut and tiny barnyard, barn, and stable were kept clean; and there was a small vegetable garden. The wife, a tall, thin, vigorous woman, sold us ten eggs for a ruble and eighty kopecks—about three times the former price. We tried to buy some honey, too; for the husband, a shrewd, bright-eyed little man, had twenty modern beehives in the field back of his hut. But we found that the hives were empty.

"There was so little clover raised last year, that the bees all starved in the winter," he said. "How can the peasants raise good crops when they have hardly any horses at all? And that is not the worst of it. Now they talk of dividing up the land—but I tell you the thriftiest peasants here will do little work until we know that we have a clear title to our farms. I won't put a finger to my plow if my land is to be taken away. And no speechifiers from Petrograd nor any of their soldiers will ever be able to make me!"

"Do all the peasants feel like you?" asked Tarasov hopefully.

"No," was the gloomy answer. "Most of them—shiftless lazy souls—think it a splendid scheme to divide. They talk and talk in the villages and there are a lot of young hooligans who raise the devil now and then. They get together in big crowds and talk and talk and shoot off guns. Two weeks ago a crowd of them came rushing up at midnight to the house of your neighbor, the Prince. They were young peasants and soldiers. They shot off their guns and bellowed like bulls. They banged on his doors, and in they went, and made a search all through his rooms. They had come to get some government papers that ought to land him in prison, they said. But what do they know of such documents? They grabbed all his papers and went away."

Soon after this we started home, stopping in at another hut to buy a huge round loaf of bread, dark brown and heavy, made of rye—called "black bread," by the Russians. This loaf and the eggs we left at home with the Finnish woman there. Already she was cooking the fish that we had bought on the river. Supper would be ready soon. Her daughter, a fresh, bright-looking girl of seventeen, had returned with the doctor some time before, and was now busily helping her mother. She was a cheery youngster. Their old master, she said, was much better now. He had been very lonely here and would be glad to have us stay, for he had been greatly worried at night ever since the raid on the Prince next door.

We decided to go, while supper was cooking, to see the old Prince and learn more of the raid. From Tarasov's cabin a path led across a small field down into a ravine, and from there up to the Prince's land. His two-story yellow frame house, weather-beaten and forlorn, stood on the bluff overlooking the river, with white birches and firs behind it. As we drew near, we caught sight of him standing motionless under the trees, a gray-headed figure in a white blouse, impassively smoking a cigarette. Although he saw us coming, he gave no sign of welcome. His greeting was wholly indifferent; his voice little more than a murmur. He shook hands in a way that seemed to say, "What does anything matter nowadays?"

He was nearly alone, he told us. All his servants had left him but one—the young widow of a soldier who had recently been killed at the front. She lived here with her three small children, and cooked for the Prince and looked after his house. He asked us to come in for a while. It was a desolate place inside. The rooms, with their stiff, ugly old chairs, tables, sofas, mirrors, all looked empty and comfortless, like mere relics of the past. The Prince had once been very gay, and there had been wild parties here of men and women from Petrograd, with music and dancing all the night. Mere memories now, the ghost of old days. He spent his time reading or walking about or staring down on the river. Under the Old Régime, he said, he had had an official position here. That was why the peasants had raided his home.

"We have come to get your accounts of our money!" they shouted, as they burst into the house. "If you are a thief, by Christ we will kill you!"

As the Prince told his story, a slight smile of amusement came upon his wrinkled face. He described how they had scowled and panted over his desk, elbowing each other aside. Soon they had gathered his papers all up and had bundled them into a burlap bag, which they had taken off to the village. He had heard nothing from them since.

"And they are our government," he remarked.

Now we were out again under the trees. He lit another cigarette and relapsed into his indifference. We left him there in the gathering dusk. Nearby, his housekeeper's little girl sat on the grass with her baby brother. Each time the wee solemn boy sat up, she would push him over again—heels over head—and the fat little boy would fairly explode with quick gasping chuckles. For him there had been no revolution, no world war. He had had excitements of his own, he had made great discoveries. Already he could sit up in the grass! Soon he would be able to walk—and would walk about for seventy years. I wondered what his awakening mind would see in the years that lay just ahead. And the millions of other small boys and girls all over Europe what would they see? Famine, pestilence and death? Or would their big brothers in every land come to the aid of all such little people and give them a new start in life?... At present he was exceedingly gay. But his chuckles were the only sound that broke the stillness of this yard. The whole place was very funereal.

## 4

Returning home, in the living room we found that the table had been laid, but supper was not ready yet. While we were waiting, my eye was caught by a spinet in the corner. Piled high with books and papers, it had escaped my attention before. It had once been a lovely old instrument, with delicate inlaid designs—but now it was cracked and broken, with the veneer fast peeling off. Some of the keys were missing, and others gave only a tinkling sound.

"My grandmother brought it here," said Juvenale Ivanovich. "A wonderful woman. Those are her books."

And he pointed to a narrow bookcase, glass enclosed, which stood in the opposite corner. Here were two or three score of books, in mellow old bindings. I noticed that most of them were in French. There was a broken set of Voltaire, and I jotted down these other titles: "Le Saint Bible." "La Russie Sous Pierre Le Grand." "Repertoire des Etranges Complete—Oeuvres de W. Scott." "Voyages Religioux en Orient, par M. L'abbé Michon." On another shelf was a full set of Shakespeare, in English, and some German magazines. Beside them were two small enameled jewel boxes, both of which were empty now. And below were several large heavy volumes entitled "La Maison Rustique." As I lifted them out, Tarasov said:

"Those are books on agriculture, published long ago in France. My grandmother used to tell me that the happiest years of her life were the two she spent as a girl in Paris. And so, when she was eager to start a fine new agriculture here, she got her books and manuals all from her beloved France. She took the methods intended for the French soil and climate, and tried to introduce them over a thousand miles to the North. Naturally, her efforts failed. But what a woman—what a woman!"

"Tell me about her," I suggested.

"It's a long story," he replied. "Let us have our supper first."

When the meal was over, he took me out behind the garden and showed me the tattered relics of what had once been a huge covered sledge. Only a few small shreds of leather and blue satin still hung upon the framework.

"This belonged to her family," he said. "See how large it was—fully twelve feet long by eight feet wide; and it was all upholstered inside. There were four wide cushioned seats that became sleeping berths at night; also a silver washstand, a narrow table for eating and a little case for books, with a mirror overhead. So they traveled in the old days. It was down in the south of Russia. She was brought up on a large estate, where there were some ten thousand serfs and household servants by the score. She had French and German governesses. When they traveled up to Moscow or went to balls at other estates, there would be three or four great sledges with eight horses hitched to each, and a Cossack guard before and behind—for there were brigands in those times. They would travel day and night. They went like the wind on the snowy road, through the forest and out over the steppe.

"When I was a little boy, often on summer evenings here my grandmother would sit with me in this old sledge, which was not so dilapidated then; and she would tell me stories of the long, long rides they took, the singing, and the sleigh-bells and the wild music of the horns. She told of fights with brigands that made my eyes pop out of my head. She told of gay parties on the estate of her father, with sixty or seventy guests who would be there for many days. She taught me nursery rhymes and songs, while I worked with her in the garden. For even now that she had come to such a humble home as this, my grandmother liked to make it gay. She planted those morning-glories that cover this end of the house; and over there in the garden, far down in the tall grass and weeds you will find her flowers growing.

"She had been brought up, as I told you, with every kind of luxury, and at the end of her long bright youth came those years in Paris. But after that her life was changed. She was one of many children; all had to be provided for. Her father had mismanaged things; his affairs had gone from bad to worse, until most of his fortune had dribbled away. So when she came back from France she found a ruined family, and when she married later on, her dowry was very small.

"She married a man in Petrograd, a noted professor of surgery in the Medical University there. The marriage was a great mistake. Within two years they both agreed that to live together longer would simply spoil the life of each one. My grandmother, however, although without religious scruples, felt that divorce was in shocking bad taste. And so, when she came with her baby, my mother, out to live in this country place, regularly once a year she went back to Petrograd to visit my grandfather there, in order to avoid any scandal.

"And in this way she lived her life—from her youth to the grave. It was very hard. Such a woman in such a rough wild region! For it was not then as it is now. On this spot a century ago was a little village of robbers, who watched like hawks for the barges loaded with rich merchandise that were bound for Petrograd. They were a regular pirate crew. Finally soldiers and police came and cleaned out this robbers' lair. Later a queer old spinstress from Petrograd bought this piece of land, built a small house and lived here alone till the time of her death. Then it was sold to my grandmother.

"My grandmother was far from practical. Though she had hardly any money at all, she bought this place without seeing it; and when she arrived she found that the buildings which had been so nicely described to her by the agent in Petrograd were largely matters of fancy. But grimly she settled down in the cabin, and here she lived for thirty-five years. She had a peasant who worked the farm, and his wife was her one servant. They lived with rigid economy. She closely studied those French books on the best methods of tilling the soil, and she did her best to apply them and make the most of her small farm. But she got barely enough to eat. They hardly ever tasted meat. She had still several trunks and chests filled with her fine Paris clothes. These she guarded carefully, and year by year she cut them up to make garments for my mother, who was no longer a baby now. Except for this companionship, my grandmother lived quite alone. After those bright years in Paris, it must have been a dreary life. The winters up here are terribly cold. I picture those nights alone in her cabin—thinking and thinking of the past.

"But she was such a true grand dame, that as time went on she made a place; the peasants all came to esteem her. In the old days down in the South, her father had stood high in the law. She had a few of his law books still. These she closely studied. And more and more she set herself to the task of seeing justice done in disputes that arose among peasants here. They were always bringing their quarrels to her. In time she became almost like a judge.

"In the meantime, her husband had died, and his small pension came to her. This made her life somewhat easier. Often when she saved a bit, she would take her daughter to Petrograd to visit friends. On one such trip, my mother grew acquainted with my father, who was an art student in the Fine Arts Academy there. He was the son of a prosperous peasant in this neighborhood—who, ambitious for his son, had sent him to the capital. My father was proud of his peasant blood, and later on he achieved fame by painting pictures of village life. Long before that, he had married my mother and I had been born. They brought me here in the summer months. And from my old grandmother, I heard her stories of the past.

"She died when I was still a small boy. My father then pulled her cabin down, and built this larger one in its place. During the rebuilding, an old sofa of my grandmother's was given by my mother to a peasant woman nearby. This woman was a newcomer here, and had never heard of my grandmother. But soon after she got the sofa, she was taking a nap upon it one day, when she saw a 'tall great lady' come into the room very silently and frown at her and say very clearly:

"'I am not pleased with you for using this sofa which was mine. I am not pleased. And nothing good will come to you, so long as you keep it here.'

"The poor woman was quite terrified; she returned the sofa forthwith. And though the ghost of my grandmother has never appeared to any one else, her spirit still lives in the minds of old people, who on festival days in the churchyard place flowers on the 'great lady's' grave.

"After the new house was built, my father resolved to stay here the year 'round and lead the life of a farmer. He bought live stock, plows and tools and hired peasant laborers. But the project met with no success, for he grew so absorbed in painting the peasants that he did not make them work. Often in the morning he would stroll out on his field, and finding a peasant he wished to paint, he would bring him back to his studio, and there they would remain all day—both of them perfectly content

"Meanwhile I was growing up, and my parents gave me a good education, sending me to Petrograd, where I specialized in chemistry. But when, at twenty-three years of age, I had left the university, I asked them to let me manage the farm. They agreed and I began at once. I was a young giant in those days; I could break a horseshoe in one hand. And the countless blunders I made at first were more than counterbalanced by my eagerness for the job. I hired some peasants and set them a pace. We worked like bulls—and within a year I had made thirty acres of land provide fodder for sixteen cattle. In the meantime I had begun to buy tools and to study modern methods adapted to this climate and soil. In the early summer, while we were still mowing the winter rye in one part of the field, we were plowing in the other part and sowing it for barley, potatoes, and cucumbers. Such haste was a perfect scandal. It made the peasants rub their eyes. But the good results they could not deny. Soon I was selling my produce to the Petrograd markets, and at last I was able to show an actual profit on the farm.

"So I worked for three or four years. Then I went back to Petrograd and entered the government service as a chemical engineer. Later I went to England and to Germany and France, and back again in Petrograd I worked for a traction company. During a period of ten years, I came here only now and then; and under the shiftless management of my big peasant neighbor, again the farm had run to seed. My parents had returned to the city. When, however, my father died in the fall of 1911, my mother and I brought his body back here. Then she returned to Petrograd, but I stayed here alone for a year and a half. At first I did this merely because I had deeply loved my father and wished to be by myself for a time. That winter I passed some strange nights in this house. My father was so strongly, so vividly before my eyes, that often it was hard to tell whether or not it was merely a dream. I had brought the mahogany bed, which had belonged to my grandmother, into my father's studio. Lying there I would talk to him as he stood at his easel; and he would talk back to me over his shoulder.

At times I felt quite cold with fear, but more often I felt nothing but a deep and quiet content. I wrote this down in full detail, for in spite of my grief my mind was clear. I closely observed each experience from a scientific point of view, and some day I shall give my records to a journal of psychiatry.[7]

"But now my passion for the land soon roused me to an active life. All winter long I worked like a peasant, repairing the house and cutting wood, getting ready my plows and other tools. In the meantime I had come to see how hard it was to improve conditions while each of us was still working alone. And so I got the first germ of my plan for cooperative work. I thought we must throw together all our separate plots of land, and buy in common the very best of agricultural machines. I worked it out in full detail with the priest and the school teacher—both of them remarkable men.

"The peasants, too, used to come to my house. They did not feel so much reserve with me as with other landowners—first, because I was the son of a peasant; and second, because I have in my breast something that makes me insanely eager to be friends with any man, woman or child. So the peasants came to me. For the making of farming implements, in my father's studio, I had lathes both for metal and wood, and the shavings and the sawdust and steel filings would accumulate and lie in heaps upon the floor. The good kind God had sent me no wife to spoil my life with her tidiness! I taught the peasants to use my tools, and some of them grew so absorbed that they would work nearly half the night. Then they wanted to know about cattle's diseases, so I got books and we studied it out. The priest used to join in these consultations, for he had a passion for horses and cattle. Slowly we made headway here. Often my peasant neighbors would ask me about my travels abroad. I would describe the farms I had seen in Germany, France and England—and also the cooperative farms in Denmark and in Sweden.[8]

"But now again I went away—for my mother, who liked the city, begged me to come back to her. So I want to Petrograd and took employment in a bank. And there I remained until the war."

---

[7] An interest in mysticism and the occult features in a number of Poole's novels, inspired by his experiences in Russia.

[8] The reforms of Chairman of the Council of Ministers Petr Stolypin (1862–1911) to promote the break-up of the communal village and abolition of repartition of land after the Revolution of 1905 began a revolution in the Russian countryside. It stimulated entrepreneurship, innovation, and the cooperative movement. Unfortunately, the force behind it weakened after the assassination of Stolypin in 1911.

# CHAPTER I

## 5

His story was interrupted by a shower of rain which drove us indoors. We went into the studio and there he resumed his narrative. Tarasov had often talked to me about the revolution—but now I asked him to give me, as clearly as he could remember it all, a coded story of what he had seen in Petrograd in the early weeks after the downfall of the Czar.

"First," he said, "I must tell you a little about my part in the war. For it throws some light upon the rest. When the war broke out, to do my share and use my skill as a chemist, I obtained work with a company which was planning munition mills in the South. Mine was laboratory work, a search for high explosives, and in the third year of the war, we were on the verge of discovering something that might have become a new force. Our little group of chemists grew terribly interested. We worked all day and often all night—and ours was hard clean thinking. We did not often feel fatigue, for by accurate computation we knew that if the damned stuff exploded too soon, we would be blown into molecules in exactly one fifty-seven-hundredth of a second. And that acted, you might say, on the brain like a glass of cognac—though at the time I was on a diet of vegetables, bread and water. At last we had what we wanted. I remember very vividly still how happy we were; I remember one night when we talked till the morning of how this terrific child of our brains would help our armies at the front.

"But for me this time was followed by a drop to deep disgust. For I was sent to Petrograd to tell of our discovery to the Government Board of Explosives there. And what a gang, a pirate crew; how different from the little group of chemists I had left behind! Here was a swarm of profiteers, who neither thought of winning the war nor of discovering anything. In their shrewd eyes you could see how they schemed to cheat both us and the government. I broke through these gray wolves at last and got in to the Artillery Board—and when they realized what we had found, it was tragic to see those expert men. They were so eager to try it out, but at the same time almost without hope. 'If only our government,' they said, 'could rid itself of these war millionaires!'

"Almost immediately after that began the revolution. I shall never forget the day that it started. I had called at the Admiralty on a certain Mr. K—, who was working on the Navy Board. He was a thick-set, middle-aged man, harsh and uncouth in his manners, and as soon as he learned of the value of our new discovery, he tried hard to force me to promise that I would have nothing to do with the Army and deal only with his Board. For the Army and the Navy were as jealous as two great cats. Finally he told me to go and see his assistant. But when I came out to the ante-room, I found it filled with officers, and at once I saw on their faces the signs of great excitement.

"'At last it has come!' one of them was exclaiming. 'What will be the result of it all?'

"Just then an older officer came in and told us what he had seen. He was coming up the Liteiny (one of Petrograd's principal streets) in one of those little American cars. It was what you call a Ford. It broke down in front of the barracks of one of our Guard regiments. While he sat waiting for his chauffeur to fix the machine, he noticed a curious agitation on the faces of the young soldiers there, who were hurrying about, bringing out rifles, cartridges and several machine guns. There was a kind of happiness and yet something solemn and tragic, too, in the eyes of all these youngsters. He asked them to help his chauffeur with the car—but after consulting together a moment, one of them came and saluted and said:

"'Your Excellency, today we are starting to make the Great Revolution—and we shall have to take your car—to carry a machine gun to use against the Czar's police. We hope you are a friend of the people and that you will not decline. We will find you a cab, your Excellency, so that you can go on your way. But please let us have your chauffeur—for we are not used to American cars.'

"He said this in a low respectful tone; and the group of young chaps standing there all seemed so very quiet, and yet so determined, too, that the officer said he felt at once that the Old Régime was done for. For this was a Regiment of the Guard! One of the soldiers got him a cab, and as he started up the street they were hoisting a machine gun into the seat of his automobile. A few moments later they passed him, all of them smiling and waving their hats. But just ahead the car broke down; and now as he passed them in his cab, it was the officer's turn to smile—while one of the young soldiers cried,

"'Your Excellency, why did you give us this car? What a car for a great revolution!'

"The officer then went on to tell how he had seen many crowds of armed men, with women and children at their sides, marching down the streets and singing. I did not wait to hear any more; I went out to see it for myself.

"The streets close by the Admiralty were as silent as the grave, but very soon as I walked along I heard a tremendous humming sound, and when I came to the great square in front of the Winter Palace, I found it like a beehive, black with swarming thousands of people and of soldiers. I made my way deep into the crowd, listening, watching, all my thoughts and feelings gripped by a force gigantic—like the world! But a new world! It was like a dream!

"Then suddenly I heard the word go 'round to burn the Palace. At once I thought of the Hermitage, which stood so close to the Palace that one could not burn without the other—the Hermitage with its Rembrandts and all its other treasures of art. My father and I had often been there. The place had been like a holy cathedral, my only religion as a child. And now, as I stood in a trance, something strange happened inside of me—and what took place I cannot recall. I remember shouting to two men to hoist me up on their shoulders. Then I began speaking to the crowd. And as I noticed that thousands of eyes were turning in my direction, I seemed to lose all consciousness. Now I was speaking down to them from somewhere in the cloudy sky.... When

# CHAPTER I

I regained my senses I was lying on the pavement. There was cool dirty snow on my face, and a soldier on his knees beside me was unbuttoning my shirt.... The Winter Palace was not burned. I do not mean in the least to say that the Hermitage was saved by my speech. That doubtless played but one little part in the thoughts and passions deep and obscure that go surging through such a multitude. I was simply a molecule in a storm.

"From there I went down the Nevsky, for I had some urgent business with a Jew at the other end. I found the big wide thoroughfare almost completely empty—no people on the sidewalks, no izvoschiks (cabbies), no trams. My Jewish friend was highly excited. 'I tell you,' he said earnestly, 'that what is happening today may change the future of the world! The Old Régime was ready to make peace with the Kaiser soon, but this change may keep the war going for years!' He knew many politicians, and his quick confused account of the chaos and alarm in those circles was indeed a contrast to the tremendous humming force of which I had just been a part. A big banker had told him that on the market all values were now breaking fast. I left him and went out again.

"More and more I had the certainty that the long expected Revolution, which in Russia had gathered its forces for fifty years, was upon us at last. I cannot express how deep it felt. The whole nation seemed to be rising here. It was as though, as I walked along, I could feel the people gathering in villages by thousands in every corner of our land.

"Suddenly, as I came 'round a corner, I saw men and women and children running toward me in scattering crowds. Not a shout nor a scream, but on they came and fled into doorways on both sides. In a moment or two, behind them I heard the rapid thud of hoofs, and then over my head the bullets began to buzz like so many bees. I looked around for a refuge, but all the doors were either closed or the doorways packed with people. I ran along close to the walls; and as the fusillade increased, I dropped on my belly. Down the street came the mounted police, firing on every side. They passed, and I heard a few groans close by—and somewhere a child began talking in a shrill excited way.

"I jumped to my feet, and running on I reached the Nicolaevsky Station.[9] It was being fired upon by police from across the square, who had installed machine guns in the windows of the Great Northern Hotel. I managed to get through the station and out onto the railroad tracks, and from there I wandered off through the poorer residence parts of the city. There was hardly a street or a courtyard where you could not hear the shots. For the revolutionists were hunting down the Czar's police, who took refuge in the houses and were driven up, floor by floor, into the attics and onto the roofs.

---

[9] The Nicolaevsky is the largest of a number of railroad stations in Petrograd, since it is the terminus of the trains from Moscow.

"Now I was near to the Neva, and as I came to one of the bridges, I saw two young servant girls coming across it with loaves of bread, skylarking along and making fun of the bullets hissing over our heads. Their excited laughter struck into me with a chill. A machine gun opened from nearby, but by now I was tired of running. I walked along in a kind of a daze. I remember meeting a sailor boy who said that the police had just seized the Admiralty. As we came near to that building, a dozen soldiers in front of us suddenly dropped on their faces. We did the same, and just in time—for the police in the Admiralty windows were getting the range very nicely. There was ice and mud in the streets, and dirty snow piles here and there. Through these we crawled or wriggled along, pretending we were wounded. So we went for nearly a mile.

"When I came at last to my mother's apartment, the servant girl who opened the door cried out when she saw me,

"'Juvenale Ivanovitch! Never in all my life did I see a chimney sweep who looked like you!'

"My clothes were torn; I was covered with mud. My mother was glad to find me alive. I had a hot bath and got into clean clothes—and then all at once with quite a shock I remembered that for five hours at least I had not smoked a cigarette. Moreover, there were none at home. I left our apartment and hurried downstairs. Out on the street I heard shots again and saw the dark shadows of soldiers. Only a few street lamps had been lit, but there was a light in a druggist's shop. I went in and asked for cigarettes. They were sold out. But in a tea shop across the street, a kindly little fellow took pity on me and gave me one.

"On my way back home, I met several soldiers with a young student in command. He was lighting a cigarette. I said, 'What a beastly business! One can't get anything to smoke.' The boy dropped his match and looked at me; he smiled in a strange sort of way and said, 'This is more a time, brother, for potassium cyanide.' The next instant he swung around on his heel, and up went his Browning—for out of the darkness came a small crowd. I could see the shine of their bayonets. A voice called, 'Are you for the Czar or against him?' There was a moment's silence then, and I was rigid as a post. In the eyes of the boy beside me I could read the question: 'Are they the Czar's provocateurs or are they real revolutionists?' He called sharply back to them, 'We are all right, brothers—come on!'

"The two groups joined and marched away. As I went home, I heard more shots and people running. I heard distant cheering, too. At home I found that the outer door to the building had been locked and barred. I pounded on it, and at last a voice from inside asked, 'Who is there?' I gave my name, and the voice then said, 'Give the number of your apartment.' I did, and the porter let me in.

"All night I heard shooting in the streets. I lay in my bed but I could not sleep. The words of Pushkin came to my mind: 'Russia can never have revolution. Russia can have only riot—merciless, bloody and senseless.' I did not dare to hope for an end of all the dissipation, intrigue, the stalling and cheating of war profiteers, the German cabal in the Court of our Czar, the tyranny of the Old Régime, the dark ignorance of the people. As I listened to the shots that night, I thought that in mobs and violence the slowly growing vision of over half a century would all go up in a smoky cloud. In the room next to mine, my old mother had lighted the little lamp in front of both her ikons, and all night I could hear her on her knees, praying,

"'O God—O Christ, our dearest brother—help our people—help them! Save them from misery, grant them success! There has been so much suffering in our land!'

"So she prayed all through the night. Toward morning I had dropped asleep; and when she came to awaken me, there was a shining look in her eyes like that of an eager happy young girl.

"'Oh, Juvenale, my dearest, I must go and see all they are doing!' she said. 'We must be careful, of course, how we go, but I feel so sure that the soldiers are good kind lads and will do us no harm.'

"I told her she must not go out, for I could still hear shooting. But then with a guilty look she explained that she had already been to the market and had talked with the people there.

"'They were all so happy,' she said, 'in a good sweet way, as though each had a solemn light in his soul, as people have during Easter prayer. Everybody looked like that—people of any class, rich or poor. Absolute strangers met each other and suddenly talked like old friends. Never in all my life did I dream there could be such friendliness in the world!' And as she spoke, there were tears in her eyes.

"I went out and tried to get news. I asked for newspapers, but people laughed. 'What a man,' they cried, not to realize that there can be no papers now!' The streets were crowded with people. They looked as they do at Easter time. I heard a young girl say gayly to another as they hurried along, 'Easter is very early this year!' And others as they passed me were singing softly, 'Christ is Risen.' Nearly all were smiling like children who are too happy to speak aloud. And I thought, 'Something really great has come. Now a new force is in the world. Now the Germans will see what we can do, when all their spies and their intrigues are swept out of Petrograd!'

"I heard workers say, 'This is no time for us to demand higher wages. Now we will work—because we are free. And until the new Russia is safe, all the wages we will ask is enough to feed our children.' I went into a milk shop, and found a strange new order there—for the customers, rich and poor, were going themselves to the milk cans, pouring out what they needed and putting down their money on the counter, careful to leave a fair amount. I grew curious and watched them close, but not one person failed to pay.

"On the streets every doorway was crowded with men and women and children watching the army trucks go by. Each truck was filled with soldiers. All the private automobiles had also been commandeered, and were filled not only with soldiers but with armed students and workingmen. Most of these fellows, who were mere boys, had the most solemn looks in their eyes. When they passed, all the people would wave and cheer, and would exclaim with tears on their faces, 'They are ours! The army is ours at last!' It was strange to see no police about. It was wonderful to see the people all so obliging, all so kind. The worst looking specimen of a man would step off the path into the wet snow to make room for a woman or a child. I felt a rising happiness. I heard a band playing the Marseillaise, I saw red flags, I saw women crying just for joy, and I noticed now that most of the men wore little red ribbons on their coats.

"Here and there on the corners were speakers who told us how to organize. They acted in place of the newspapers now; they told us what was being done and called on every one to aid. They were forming militia police to keep order, and organizing the food supplies, finding where food was needed most and how it should be distributed to every quarter of the town. They formed committees in each house, and a larger committee for each block, and these committees ascertained the needs of every family. Every one was trying to help. Real work and a boundless bright good will flowed like waves from all the streets up into every room in the town. It was one of those vast miracles that come to a nation only at moments.

"If only such a mighty force could be guided right, I thought, and spread all over Russia, out to every town and village. Now was a time for thinking of larger things than food for ourselves. And because for so many years I had been absorbed in the peasants, searching for some way to settle the greatest of all Russian problems—how the land could be made to yield better lives to the people—my mind came back to this question now. This was like a tremendous rock, sharp and ugly, underneath all these smiles and happy songs. It must be clearly seen at once, it must be answered with a plan—or soon it would rise slowly up and split the whole revolution apart.

"So I called on a friend, an engineer, and asked if he thought it was possible to tell the new government my plan. He answered, 'Now any new idea will be gladly welcomed, brother. Today you can work any miracle in Russia, for I tell you our country has been born anew!' He advised me to put it in writing first. I went home, and all that day and night I drew up my plan for land reform. The next day I called upon the new Minister of Agriculture, who had just been appointed in the Provisional Government. He had a fine strong, intelligent face; he was a university man well known for his knowledge of farming. He said that he would consider my plan.

"'But remember,' he told me with a smile, 'that we cannot do everything all at once. For the city is full of men like you, in their rooms day and night, each drawing a plan for Russia.' Anxiety came into his eyes. 'I fear it will be hard,' he said. 'For politics will soon come in. There are so many Russians who have been accustomed to attack the government. This life-long habit will not change, and soon they will be attacking us. They will be impatient, they will not wait, they will shout to us, "Do something! Do something—for the love of Christ!" But when we ask them what to do, we shall find them all impractical. They have been negative all their lives, and they

# CHAPTER I

cannot be positive even now. They are not builders—only planners—each with his theory or his plan, and holding to it like grim death.'

"I went away anxious and depressed, for I feared the Minister was right, and that this ecstatic mood of the people would soon be broken in quarrels, without any practical good accomplished. Now was the time without delay to do real work, get it started at once!

"My thoughts kept centering on the soil. Surely the peasants must have more land, but it would be a crime to the nation to give them soil they could not till—for then it would lie idle, crops would fail and famine set in. They must have better plows and tools, and tractors to replace the horses which had been taken by the war. To give them such machinery, and teach than how better to till the soil, it was my purpose to make use of the cooperative societies that exist by tens of thousands in our Russian villages. They are groups for purchasing only. I wanted them for production, too. Not only should they buy machines; they should also throw together their land, farm it all together in a modern scientific way under expert guidance, and then divide the produce in shares according to what each one had put in. To stimulate this, I wished the authorities to proclaim that they would sell plows and tractors only to such groups as these, and that only to such peasants would the government give more land.

"Of course, to get all this machinery would involve a vast expense, but I felt we could get it from abroad—most of it from America. Moreover, many munitions plants in Russia might be adapted to turn out plows and tractors. But who should teach the peasants how to use these new machines? That, too, was included in my plan. I wanted the new government to seize the opportunity, while all the people in the towns were in this exalted state, to enlist tens of thousands of workingmen of the more intelligent kind, who should not only make the machines but follow them to the villages and show the peasants how they were worked.

"In the dreams I had in those days, I saw great caterpillar plows, crawling, crawling everywhere through the meadows and waste lands of Russia, crushing down small trees and bushes, turning up black furrows of earth. Food in plenty for every man! And that was my revolution! I saw the peasants banding together in cooperative groups that should be like a million corner-stones on which a new nation was to rise. And my plan was practical! I saw the tractor forcing them to work together instead of apart, forcing the lazy peasants to keep up with the pace of others—for the tractor would not wait. It would force each man to do his share, and there could be no shirking. The thing would work because it must!

"I say my plan was practical! I talked to the peasants by hundreds, who began to pour into the city to take part in the revolution, and from them, without exception, I got warm approval for my scheme. But the new political leaders were by no means so favorable. Again and again they put me off; they had no time for such real things. They kept quoting books to me. One of them smiled in a lofty way and said, 'Your scheme is old. It was tried long ago by the Brook Farm group in America. And it failed, brother, it failed.' The fool! What did that group of American writers know about caterpillar plows? But I could not convince him. Another leader, a ponderous chap, carefully thought it over and said, 'Tractors give no manure, my friend—and without manure what good is a farm?'

"It was tragic in Petrograd, the lack of organizing force—or rather, the way such force was spoiled and hindered by the theoreticians scattered about all over the town. In our apartment building, where there were thirty-four families, I said, 'Let us stop sending thirty-four servant girls out each day to the bread lines. Let us combine and send two or three to get the bread for all of us.' But one tall solemn fellow replied, 'In this time of our new-found liberty, each should be free to follow his taste. Some like one bread shop more than another.' And to defend such liberty, he went about the building, talking against my little idea, until the people turned it down. Then I made another suggestion. We were afraid robbers might break in, for we knew that many jails had been opened. 'Let's organize our defense,' I proposed. 'Let all the men in the building take turns in standing guard below.' But the Solemn One argued against this, too, as a sacrilege to the revolution. 'Why should we guard our belongings,' he asked, 'when Russia is one great brotherhood now? Any man can have my property.' It happened that the very next night a sneak-thief got up to the attic and stole a shirt which was hanging to dry. And it belonged to the Solemn One. When he heard of his loss, he said pompously, 'Plainly some brother is more in need of clean linen than I.' I looked at him and doubted it.

"So went the revolution. If you in America ever feel that your practical ways are a curse to your country and should be destructed, all that you will need to do is to send some ships to Russia, fill them up with our theoreticians and then let the ships set sail for your shores! But while you are swallowing such human pills, for the love of God load those same ships down with your practical men—the honest ones—and send them over here to us. And whatever our theoreticians may say against your 'bourgeois Yankee land,' be sure that the mass of us Russians will welcome such Americans!

"As you go about in Russia now, you will find countless men like me who are bitter, terribly bitter, against the whole new government. We are bitter because of the chance that was lost. We are bitter because of the happiness, the immense and amazing happiness, of those first weeks of the revolution. Whatever comes of it after this, every one in the world should be plainly told of what took place in those days and nights. For it was a dazzling revelation of the deep, deep powers for brotherhood and friendliness that lie buried in mankind. I was no dreamer; I was a chemist, a scientist used to dealing with facts. All my life I had smiled at social dreams as nothing but Utopias. But in those days I was wholly changed, for I could feel beneath my feet this brotherhood like solid ground. There is no end to what men can do—for there is no limit to their good will, if only they can be shown the way.

"But it was not shown in Petrograd. The real things were left undone. The army was not gripped in time. Still worse, by foolish orders abolishing 'le peine de mort' and bidding ignorant soldiers to elect their officers, twelve million armed men, mostly young peasants, instantly became a horde—a mob that cried for peace and land. And the government gave them neither one. To give both was not necessary. If by deeds the government had convinced them that it meant to give them land, I believe these peasants would have said, 'Now at last we have something real. For this we must fight against Berlin, or the Kaiser will try to grab what is ours.' But the government did nothing but talk. And so the sharp ugly rock from below, which I who am a peasant's son had felt at the very start, began to appear rising slowly up through all the empty speeches. Peasants by hundreds, then by thousands, came pouring into Petrograd—old peasants from the villages, young peasants from the army—all insisting, 'Give us land!' And on this the government split apart.

"For the bourgeois leaders stood by the landowners; the socialists, by the peasants. The Soviet soon seized control. Now all was quarrels, class against class, and bitterness and cries for revenge. One day I went to the Tauride Palace, where at that time the big Soviet (the Council of Soldiers and Workers) was meeting. One regiment after another came marching up to the building, and stopped and swore allegiance. There were red flags and banners. There was a tremendous multitude reaching as far as you could see. From a distance they seemed like one great force; but when you drew close and mingled among them, you saw the angry passions in the individual eyes. Some soldiers had brought there under arrest an old official of the Czar. They were beating him on the back with their guns, and calling him a slave and a spy. I shall never forget his look of terror, and his gray head bobbed down at each blow. The people all around us looked at him with such hatred it gave me a sinking fear. What a change from that first week! And what was the cause? Uncertainty. Nothing practical had been done, and so had come chaos and distrust. I went into the old Palace and found it packed with people. The halls were filled with dirt and refuse. They had been crowded day and night, and looked as though they had been invaded by uncouth barbaric hordes. I began to lose faith in the revolution.

"On another day I was on my way to the Minister of Railroads, to talk to him about my plan. On the street my cab was stopped by crowds of people marching, waving banners, shouting, 'Death to all servants of the Czar! Let the government hang them all! Down with the rich capitalists! Give the factories and the mills to the workers, and to the peasants give the land!' They were singing the Marseillaise, these dirty, tired men and women—singing it in an angry way with harsh discord of voices. Shouts kept rising from the throng. And I blamed the politicians for this! At a time when Russia had the chance to realize that great freedom for which the nation had been groping blindly for some fifty years, what a shame it was for the leaders to rouse such angry passions!

"I came to the home of the Minister. He was out, but I saw his wife and gave her all the blueprints and memoranda of my plan. I wished to make use of the thousands of locomotives now out of repair, to adapt them for what we farmers call 'double engine steam plowing' on the land. From there I went to my former friend, the Minister of Agriculture. But again he put me off. The government, he said, would consider my scheme very carefully; but first they must get the political organization all complete. I warned him of the need of haste.

"'The peasants,' I cried, 'are demanding all the land of the private estates. And this will split all Russia apart into owners and peasants—it means civil war!' I urged my plan as a compromise.

"So it was day after day. I went from one Ministry to another. Everywhere my efforts failed. But if the leaders in the towns were deaf to any sensible scheme, it was not so with the peasants themselves. In that fever of talk in Petrograd, I received a message one day in May from the village here. And it came like a fresh wind of hope. A peasant in this neighborhood, who all his life had worked and saved until now he had as much land as I, wrote to me on the behalf of himself and two other peasants.

"'Barin,' he wrote, 'you were quite a prophet. Last summer you said we must throw together all our lands and property, and buy the best machinery and work the land together on shares. Now the time has come to do it, for the revolution is here. In Petrograd they only talk; here we want to see something done. So we three and our sons had a meeting, and we decided the thing must be done in such a way that no one can shirk his share of the labor. Besides, it is hard to figure what share of the profits each shall have. Please come and help us.'

"So I came back to the village and met these shrewd honest neighbors of mine. And what a relief from Petrograd! Real work, real life! We figured for days—everything cautious—feeling our way. The peasant must see every step. By the amount of land and the number of horses, the number of plows, the amount of manure, which each put in, we tried to reckon out what should be his share of the proceeds. No visionary brotherhood here, but good sound brotherhood all the same, for the mutual benefit of all. We also had to figure out the proportion of labor done by each. One of the peasants had a son whose left arm had been lost in the war; another had no sons at all, but his daughter helped him in the field; while the third, who had two sons at the front, had still another, a lad of sixteen. Now whose labor was worth the most—the boy of sixteen, the grown daughter, or the man who had lost one arm?

"Before you Americans get too angry with Russia for not doing our share, you should ask yourselves first, 'Has any American village been stripped so terribly bare of its sons?' And before you decide we are nothing but dreamers, you should come to our villagers and see how shrewd and sensible many Russian peasants are. I did not say they are all like that. There are lazy shiftless peasants, like the one that I showed you today; and there is a dense awful ignorance and poverty throughout the land; everywhere there is need of good schools. But in every village you will find men like my three partners—and on them the hope of Russia hangs. If we throw our land together, buy modern plows and tractors, seeds, and use the best methods on the soil, the neighbors will watch and will follow our lead just so soon as they can see an actual profit from our work.

"For the peasants are cautious, mere words won't do. Mere words, it is true, can sometimes make them rise in fury and riot and burn. But in their hard slow daily lives, you must prove every new thing to them first. This we shall do, and then we shall help them to organize other groups like ours.

"But it cannot be done at once. As I told you, with my three partners I carefully figured for many days. Then I went back to Petrograd to try to raise a small fund for our work, and buy machines. I had no success. Later, the bank where I was employed shifted me to their Moscow branch. And meanwhile my partners decided to wait until my return. One of them, the poorest one, is the little chap I showed you today, the fellow with the beehives. The second is an old school-teacher here, like me the son of a peasant. The third is running my larger farm. We shall go and talk with him some day. Later we shall talk with the teacher. I want you to hear and see for yourself."

# 6

Tarasov had talked on and on till now it was very late at night. Several times he had stopped short, for there had been shots from the river; and remembering the raid on the old Prince two weeks before, he had taken his rifle down from the wall, and then gone on with his narrative. Now we heard quite a fusillade, and shots and distant peals of laughter, angry cries.

"It's the hooligans down on the river," he said. "I think it means nothing—but in case it should, I shall let you have my Browning, while I keep the rifle downstairs."

"No, thanks," I replied. In various little mix-ups, I have learned it is better to be unarmed. I was now very tired and drowsy. I climbed to my small attic room, threw off my clothes and got into bed. Through the open window I could hear boats passing below, with voices singing, laughing, talking. I heard an accordion playing a gay little air, and the barking of dogs, and still a few shots now and then. I was nearly asleep when suddenly, from the river just beneath my window, came a deep mellow bellowing voice. The cry was taken up at once from across the river, then farther down, and I heard it caught up again and again and repeated far off in the distance. Silence for perhaps ten minutes. Then the same bellowing voice again, and again the answer calls.

"What's he trying to do?" I asked, with the peevish irritation of a man half dead for sleep. "Get together the crowd for another raid?" Again the bellow. "Damn him, why can't we *all* go to sleep tonight?"

Then with a little rush of relief I remembered what Tarasov had told me in his descriptions of river life. The man below was a watchman, guarding the logs on the river bank; and as had been done for centuries, so now at intervals all through the night he would call to the watchman across the river, who in turn would call to the man on this side a mile farther down. So the voices would zig-zag back and forth, and travel off into the distance.

A queer old custom. I remembered Chinese cities where I had heard such watchmen's calls. What a strange country Russia was, midway between the East and the West. Tarasov could talk all he liked about his shrewd practical peasants and his sensible little plan. They were deeper than that, these Russians, mysterious as the Far East. On the other hand, how human they were! Thank God, I was right in the heart of them now.

It was good to be in the country.

# Chapter II

## I

The days and nights that followed were spent tramping about the countryside and visiting the huts of peasants in the little hamlets scattered through the neighborhood, often less than a mile apart. After an early breakfast, the Finnish cook would ask us at what time we wanted lunch. "Oh, about four or five o'clock," Tarasov would inform her. But as a rule we would not return until very late in the evening. After a few such experiences, the eyes of the Finnish woman grew grim, and she gave up preparing meals only to have them insulted. Her daughter was friendly to us still. She would serve our breakfast at seven o'clock, and when she went to bed at night she would leave the samovar boiling, so that we could make tea if we liked.

But mother and daughter had all they could do to look after the house and nurse their old master, who was slow in recovering. One of them sat up with him every night, for he was afraid to be left alone, and sometimes I would see the young girl reading to him in the garden. A heavy, feeble figure, he sat there wrapped in an old green rug, with a brown silk cap upon his head. Like his neighbor, the Prince next door, he had been wrecked by the revolution. His factory in Petrograd had been seized by his workers, who were now trying to run it themselves. The winter was not far ahead. What would become of this old man? He did not seem to care very much, nor did he want to talk to us. He merely repeated two or three times,

"It is good to have you in the house. It is good to hear your steps at night."

But for the most part he kept to his room. Moreover, he was but a tenant here. And as Tarasov filled in for me the warm memories of this home of his boyhood, his grandmother, his parents and friends, these figures emerging from the past would crowd out the present tragedy.

Day by day the big log cabin, with the giant fir tree behind it, the maples, little pines and birches reaching down to the riverside, assumed a familiar look to my eyes. For all its unkempt scragginess, the place had a homelike personal air. And I grew to know the neighborhood, where we roamed about as our fancy willed. No regular hours, no regular meals. Just a snack now and then in some peasant's hut; for the housewives were hospitable. During the meal there would be much talk, and after that we would wander off into the fields or into a wood, and there sit down to fill in my notes. It was a beautiful country. Through the ripening oats and rye, white daisies and buttercups raised their heads. The river ran between high banks with yawning quarries and ravines, and behind was a rolling country of fields and woods and gullies, orchards, stacks of hay and straw, long crooked fences made of poles. Narrow dirt roads wound about like paths, and over these roads came small carts and tiny hay ricks drawn by ponies. Peasant men and women and children passed Tarasov's cabin at all hours, day and night. A few wore boots of leather or bark, but most of them went barefoot, and at night in the darkness they would flit by without a sound.

There was mystery in this country. It had many old traditions and myths reaching back for thousands of years. Across the river on a hill was a half-ruined monastery. Once it had been a great fortified place, to repel the Swedish invaders; and for escape in time of need, the doughty monks of those early days had dug a tunnel under the river. This tunnel came up on the opposite side in a dark cave in the depths of a quarry. Small boys would explore it fearsomely.

Things were still very primitive here. The hamlets on our side of the river were forlorn little clusters of huts, with the heavy straw-thatched roofs often rotting to decay. Small meager vegetable gardens, rooks calling sleepily in the trees, lean prowling dogs and filthy pigs, dilapidated chickens. Only the white geese seemed to flourish. Large and plump and spotlessly clean, they made a bright contrast to the rest. Dirt, refuse and poverty. The housewife who would be tidy had no easy time of it. The brooms they used were simply round bundles of twigs bound onto sticks. The stables were built right onto the huts. Horses, pigs and cattle, all lodged close to the people, and the strong smells of the animals came into the kitchens. Swarms of flies were everywhere. There were strips of rag carpet on the floors, and I saw a few looms and spinning wheels. Although most of the children looked ruddy and strong, I saw many gaunt little urchins about, some pitifully white and weak. I noticed how many had bad teeth. We kept meeting people, young and old, whose aching jaws were bound up in old cloths.

Here life was hard and meager. Now and then we would find a new hut, poorly built and very small, and we would learn that it belonged to a newly married couple—often they were mere boy and girl. So they started their homes; and the end could be seen in huts a little larger, but very dirty, very old, that looked weighed down by trouble. These people worked from early to late. They would start for their fields at daylight, and the evening would find them still toiling there, for it was light until nine o'clock. We would find whole families working.

I remember one such group, of a dozen men, women and children, scattered over a big square field. A small boy of six or seven was coming out from the village nearby with a heavy iron kettle and an enormous loaf of black bread. Red-faced and breathing hard, he was trudging toward a woman who had built a fire of fagots. Tea and bread was to be their lunch. We stopped the little urchin, and I gave him a few pieces of candy from a store, which I kept in my pocket for the benefit of such as he. It caused acute excitement. Dropping the kettle and the bread, he rushed here and

# CHAPTER II

there over the field showing his great treasures to all. The other children were after him now, and soon the sweets were divided. Then quickly the excitement died, and the dull monotonous labor went on.

This field, like most of those in the district, was a strange sight to a foreigner. The land was divided in long thin strips of light green, yellow and silver gray, of oats and barley, flax and rye, with border of weeds and thistles between. For the village, in this neighborhood, held the land in common, and about once in twenty years the village Mir would meet and argue for hours and hours, day after day, and would at last re-apportion the land according to the number of men and boys in each family. Each would get a few thin strips, to hold and till for the next generation. This old Russian system of land holding still prevailed throughout most of the country, but as in many parts, so here, there were villages that had given up the plan of common ownership and had permanently divided the land into fields of a few acres each, to be held as private property. Tarasov had urged this change upon them. There had been endless waste, he said, in the former system which gave to each peasant three or four tiny strips of land, some of them barely ten feet wide, in different parts of the neighborhood. It made any improvement in tilling the soil practically impossible.[1]

## 2

One day, about two miles from his home, he brought me to his larger farm. Close by, on the adjoining land, was a log dwelling with stables and barns, where lived the peasant who had written to Tarasov in Petrograd urging him to come and help in the new co-operative plan. For several years this peasant had worked Tarasov's farm on shares. My friend had bought an American plow and they had tried the deeper plowing with great success. Their rye and barley grew rich and high, as compared to that on neighboring fields where the crops were low and sparse. Today the peasant was out on a field with a plow and a team of horses. His wife was a large, strong woman about fifty years old but still in her prime, with kindly vigorous features. She gave us a warm welcome, and in the small garden behind the hut, she served us milk in an earthenware bowl and a huge chunk of fresh black bread. Then came a brown pudding and after that fresh cucumbers. Her five small grandchildren romping about did not seem to bother her.

---

[1] This village was practicing the old system of repartitional tenure, that is redividing the land to families, based on the number of males in the household, every twenty years or so. The Stolypin reform was aimed at eliminating this practice in favor of ownership of a sector of the village lands permanently.

"She never worries," Tarasov said, "nor have I ever seen her sit down. She works with such a look of quiet and good-natured peace that you would swear she was sitting in a very easy chair. But no, she is either cooking or cleaning the house or washing the clothes."

"And the mending," I suggested. "Does she darn stockings standing up?" Juvenale Ivanovich scowled at me.

"You are always picking flaws," he said. "Don't you like my country?"

"Tremendously—and most of all because of the way your writers have of sticking to the truth about life. But ever since you brought me here you have tried to idealize. I tell you I'm going to write it all exactly as I see it. It's wonderful enough as it is. I like that woman and I'm glad she has sense enough to *sit down* with the socks."

"All right," he snapped. And we drank our tea.

The peasant came in from his work. He was short-legged, big-shouldered, strong as a bull, with a broad bearded face and wrinkled skin, and he had little bright blue eyes. After his greeting he turned at once to the question of the land. He was anxious to learn from Tarasov how the Provisional Government was planning to divide it up.

"Will they take all the land in this district," he asked, "and divide it among the peasants here? Or will they take all the land in the province, and give a piece to every one? If they do, there will be little for each, because then every idle loafer in the large towns will come in for his share." The peasant's heavy face contracted. "Sometimes I stop my plow on the field, and my horses wait, and I ask myself, 'Why should I waste my labor, my manure and seed on this land, which may be taken away from me and given all to strangers?'" He fell silent and stared down at his hands, which were trembling slightly now. Tarasov turned to me and said,

"This farm is his passion, it is like his child. I have seen him take up the earth in his hand and taste it, to judge of its quality. In no other country in the world have the peasants such a love for the soil."

Now the man began to talk of the plan for a cooperative. He had thought it over all summer, he said, and there were some questions he wanted to ask. Soon they were discussing the endless obstacles in the way. The peasant's mind returned again to his one great anxiety.

"Even if we work out our plan, and get all the land to the last square foot under fine cultivation," he said, "what will stop our neighbors from asking the Starosta (village elder) to call together the Mir and divide the land all over again?[2] Then they will get the results of our work, while they themselves have done nothing but open wide their hairy throats. I tell you I must be sure of my land; I must have a full title, drawn up in the town. I must know that every day I work will benefit my grandchildren. As it is, I do not own my farm. It is mine perhaps for twenty years, but it is owned by the

---

[2] *Mir* in Russian has various meanings: the world, peace, and in this case the village acting as a regulating body under an elder or *starosta*.

village. And that is very bad for me. I want to feel that always I can do what I like with it. If I want to sell it—all right, I can. If I want to join this cooperative plan of yours—all right, I can, but even then I must have a full title to my shares, so that I can sell if I like. They must be mine—that's what I mean. I must no longer be a slave to every loafer around me."

Then all at once his small blue eyes flashed out in a surprising way, as though at sight of a promised land. For Tarasov was describing how with a caterpillar plow they could transform the countryside, bring all the waste areas into use and so provide good land for all. There would be no question of seizure then, for there would be enough for each. The tractor was the blind prophet of steel that would lead them out of the wilderness. The peasant listened intently.

"Once I went to Petrograd," he said in a low eager tone. "I went there by the railroad. And on the train I thought to myself, 'Suppose that we had forty big plows all dragged by such an engine as this—how we would tear through the bushes and stumps, how we would cut through the virgin soil!' Yes, that is what we surely need—harrows and plows and the power to drive them! My one horse went so slowly that all my farm work was held back; but since you lent me your big new plow, I have borrowed another horse; and often I will drive the team as fast as I can make them go, for the fun of seeing such a big furrow roll up from the soil like a miracle. And I hear that in America they have a machine so wonderful that it plows and harrows all at once." He glanced from Tarasov over to me. "Your American friend must think us a very one-horse people," he said. "Once I saw a picture of New York. The buildings there go up into the clouds." He was silent, then drew a hungry breath. "And what machines they have for farms!

"But things are very hard for us here," he went on, in a tone of sadness. "The workmen in the cities are getting enormous wages now, and I learn from the men on the barges that some get as high as twenty-five rubles for one day's work. And yet while all those others get rich, the government still keeps down by law the price at which we can sell our grain. I can save nothing. Often I even lose on a field. And so it has been with all of us. We have had to eke out our farming by working for the landowners.

"One owner told me last winter that if I would guard his forest against theft of wood by the peasants, I could pasture my cattle there this summer. So I did—but what is the result? One of my cows was eaten up by a bear this week in those same woods. They say that a cow with a bell on her neck is never lost. And they were right about the bell; it was not lost; it was on the ground. But all the rest of my cow was gone." The peasant heaved a heavy sigh. "And how well I guarded that forest last winter. I used to creep along on my snowshoes up to some place where I could hear chopping. Then I would up with my shot-gun. 'Hands up!' I would cry. The timber thief would call back to me, 'Oh, my good neighbor, don't you know that this forest belongs to God? It should be free for all of us, brother!' But I would keep my shotgun up. 'Take your ax and go away!' I would cry. That is how well I guarded the wood. But now my cow is eaten, and so all my labor went into the bear.

"Since then, things have gone from bad to worse. For this district of twenty villages, we have only two policemen—and, with all the theft by hooligans, what can two policemen do?... But so it is. So it is with us here. Well, tell me something about the war—for I don't see any newspapers now."

"It is bad enough," Tarasov said, and he gave a brief account of the retreat at Tarnopol—whole divisions of troops in panic, leaving supplies and munitions behind them, abandoning their heavy guns. The peasant listened dismally.

"And now all those big guns are lost? Oh, that is bad!" He shook his head. "I was once myself a soldier; and I know that for an army it is far better to be without boots than without artillery." He brooded for a moment. From a big lump of sugar he nibbled off a tiny piece, then drank his tea and let it sweeten in his mouth; for in this way the sugar seemed to go further.

"I hear no more from my three sons," he continued quietly. "I think they are still at the front. The last time I heard from one of them, he was in a hospital. He had been wounded three times, he wrote, and besides his legs were twisted up by rheumatism from the trenches. Where he is now, I do not know. And the other two? Alive or dead? We never hear." He said this without the slightest change of expression on his broad, hairy face.[3]

"When the war began," he went on, "my two married sons left their families with me. Their wives now work in the district town and we keep the children here—four girls and a boy. I am wondering how it will be with them when it comes to dividing up the land. It should not be done in the old way, according to the number of boys in every peasant family. The girls, too, should be counted in. I look at my granddaughters and think, 'Oh, you poor little creatures. You will be obliged to hunt for a husband before you can get any land. And without land there is no bread.' As things now stand, a woman who bears only girls can bring a family to starvation. They should be treated all alike. Each family should be given land according to the number of children—the mouths to be fed. For this is right.

"And they should have better schooling, too. Of what use is it to our children to have city teachers who think that bread grows on the trees? We don't want fine ladies and gentlemen to educate our girls and boys. If by a miracle of the saints such people were robbed of all their wealth, we are quite sure that they would starve; for they know nothing of tilling the soil or of building a hut or of spinning flax. We want the kind of teachers who, if they were robbed and stripped naked here, would know how to begin their lives again and in a year be prosperous. Such teachers we want for our children. We should have them all over Russia."

---

[3] One of the aggravations for Russians that caused opposition to the war and support for ending it was the poor communication on what was happening to family members at the front. They often did not hear for months that family members had become casualties.

## CHAPTER II

The peasant sat impassive, with his brown gnarled hands on his knees, staring vainly down the road. I noticed the hard muscular limbs that showed beneath his blue cotton blouse. He had lived his whole life in this neighborhood. I was struck by that phrase, "all over Russia." What did he know of Russia, stretching out over a sixth of the globe? As he looked off down the road, it seemed to me that he saw this village and perhaps the next one, in his fancy, and other localities nearby, certain roads and woods and fields that were familiar to his eye, and the river banks and the river itself murmuring off toward the city. Out farther outlines all grew faint. Beyond for him lay only rumor—a vague dim land of hearsay, myth and fable, superstition.

The dusk was slowly deepening now. We went in to have a look at his house, and I found it clean and homelike. In the little living-room, in a queer old hanging cradle swinging slightly to and fro, lay their tiny grandson.

"He is the son of a soldier," his grandmother said quietly, "and he will be a soldier, too." Tarasov replied that perhaps by that time there would be no need of soldiers. But she sighed and shook her head. "That will never be possible," she declared.

I noticed an "ikon" on the wall, with a candle burning in front of it. Close by hung a chromo picture of a Russian bear hunt and another of a garden scene with gallants of an age gone by, somewhere down in Italy. There was, too, a picture here which I have seen in farmers' homes in many lands, the one entitled, "A Man's Life from the Cradle to the Grave." We went into the kitchen, and there the woman showed to me her huge brick stove. It had been freshly whitewashed. She showed me the holes where boots were dried, and the long cavernous oven, in which, when a wood fire had burned till the bricks were thoroughly heated, the fire was then raked away and the loaves went in. Here she could bake for five hours after the fire had gone out. And besides, in winter it warmed the whole house.

Her grandchildren had finished their suppers, and now, as it was Saturday night, she undressed them for their weekly baths. One by one, wrapped tight in a quilt, the small girls were carried out to the bath house, a tiny log hut filled with steam, there to be thoroughly steamed and scrubbed, for that was the usual custom. On our way home, through each village we passed, we saw children being hustled out, wrapped in quilts and blankets. Almost every peasant hut had its own little bath house close by.

I shall long remember something I saw in a lonely hamlet that evening. On either side of the narrow dirt road was a row of half a dozen huts. In the deepening dusk it was silent, except for low voices from indoors, and the poverty and the loneliness seemed to weigh down like a pall. Over fifteen miles from a railroad, how could the revolution penetrate to such a spot? And if Russia were a nation of just such little hamlets, what hope of gathering them all into a great self-government?

We found a peasant there, all alone, scowling at two proclamations nailed to the log wall of a barn. One had been put up months before, a printed sheet now stained and torn by the weather. It had been sent out from Petrograd, by the socialist Peasants' Council, urging the peasants everywhere to help in nationalizing the land.

The other proclamation, laboriously written with pen and ink, was more recent and was a local affair. It was twice the size of the other one, for on it had been awkwardly written the names of over three hundred peasants, not only men but women, too, who lived in the neighboring villages. There was added the age and the occupation of each, and the amount of land he held. Here were the new voters of the Russian republic: a republic still unborn, for no elections had yet been held. But on the other half of the sheet was a list of a dozen candidates, and it was announced that the first election would take place the following month, in a certain village schoolhouse.

"You must think over carefully all these candidates," read the announcement, "so that when you come together, each one of you will have decided which are the ones he wants to elect."

At all this the peasant beside us was scowling in a puzzled way. We asked him what he thought of it.

"Well," he answered slowly, "we must have this meeting. We must have it because we need more land. But how we are to do it, God knows."

We left him standing in the dusk. And as we walked home I had a feeling that in numberless hamlets like this, silent places, mere specks in that boundless land of the North, other lonely figures were standing in the dusk that night, uncouth and silent, puzzling, trying to read the signs of the times, straining their eyes for a glimpse of the dawn. But the dawn was not yet. The dusk slowly deepened. Night was settling over the land.

# 3

As we tramped about the countryside, I came to notice more and more what a part the river played in the lives of the people. With the railroad many miles distant, the river was their highway still. Instead of coming to watch the trains, the peasants came to the village dock where the steamer stopped every morning and night. Here they got their news of the world. And besides, with the fishing and logging, the sawmills and the quarries, the river helped them to eke out their hard living on the land.

I never tired of watching the ever-changing river life. On our walks we would often stop to watch the stout women, girls and boys, loading stove wood and big blocks of limestone onto barges. There were always peasants fishing here, patient stolid figures kneeling in their rude canoes, dugouts hewn from poplar logs, working as a rule in pairs with a long coarse net between them. And at all hours day and night the great rafts and barges passed. At night I would see their slow moving red lights and would listen to the voices coming up out of the hazy dark, talking, laughing, singing.

## CHAPTER II

Beneath rose the mysterious voice of the deep, soft stream, as it swirled along on its way to the distant city.

It carried my thoughts to Petrograd. There in the feverish days of July, when the Bolsheviks were trying to seize the government, one morning I saw a riderless horse come tearing around a corner, snorting blood, shot through the neck, and as it galloped along a canal, a big black-bearded peasant on a barge piled high with wood rose slowly up from a pit in the logs and scowled about in a puzzled way, while from not far off there came the rattle of a machine gun. I wondered what he was thinking of this city revolution, the shouting crowds, the volleys of shots, the armored cars that were racing by with shrill screams of warning. For so much depended on what he thought, this man who had come floating down from the boundless fields and forests where the great mass of the Russians dwell. Of the attitude of such as he, toward the city and the changes there, I gathered many impressions now from various different angles.

We stopped for dinner, one Sunday, in a hut close down to the water-side. In the village nearby, church was just over, and the peasants were flocking home: the men in their somber Sunday suits of black or gray, the women in white or colors, with gay kerchiefs over their heads. The bank was low and sloping here, and a narrow field extended up from behind the hut, while in front of it fishing nets were spread, and there were oars and boat-hooks and coils of rope hanging up to dry. The wife was strong and capable, with reddish hair, a freckled face and bright honest friendly eyes. She had not been to church, she said, but out on the river fishing. She showed us the seven big fish she had caught. For each one she would receive seven rubles in the market—forty-nine rubles for two hours' work!

"But then I stopped," she said with a smile, "for what is the good of money, these days?" Besides, this was a holiday. Soon her relatives would drop in, and she wanted to cook a nice dinner first. While she moved about her kitchen she talked of the high prices. In Petrograd the price of stove wood rose each week; and this, she said, was partly because the peasant boys and women here demanded such big wages for loading the wood onto barges.[4]

"They hardly know what to ask," she laughed. "It is like a game. Every week they keep asking more, and always they get it, and so we go on. And so long as things are in such a state, why should not our people get all they can? Petrograd got all the profits once, and always it was at our expense. Now our turn has come. Why shouldn't we take it?

"Yes, we are living pretty well," she continued quietly, "in spite of the disorders in towns. We have plenty to eat, for we catch our own fish, raise our own chickens, our wheat and rye and vegetables. As for clothes, in almost every hut we have old looms

---

[4] Perhaps a more important problem was a shortage of horses to haul the wood out of the forests, so many having been taken for the army and then lost in combat.

and spinning wheels that we have not used for years—but now all the old grannies are fixing them up. We grew flax in our fields this summer; there are still enough sheep to give us some wool, and so this winter we'll make our own clothes."

Her log hut was fresh and clean. The small living room had heavy beams supporting the low ceiling. The wide brown planks of the floor were polished from much scrubbing. The partition walls were painted blue, and so were the doors and the cupboards built into the corners. There were flowered plants in the little windows. I saw a Singer sewing machine.[5] Certainly they had prospered here. They not only farmed and fished; her husband was the foreman of a logging gang on the river. They had no children, but on one wall hung a photograph of a young officer with his wife and baby. He was their nephew, Tarasov said. He had been badly wounded and was home on leave. On his gray jacket, which hung by the door, were pinned a medal and three Crosses of St. George, for the boy had distinguished himself during the great Brusilov drive down into the Carpathians. It was there he had won his commission.

Soon he limped in from the garden, a lean sinewy lad of about twenty-two. He was dressed in gray uniform trousers and a soft yellow linen blouse with a sash around the waist. His face was gaunt, with high cheek-bones, a light mustache and clear, steady blue eyes. Although friendly enough in his greeting, he did not seem to care to talk. His young wife had come in behind him, with their baby, which she gave him to hold while she spread a blue checkered cloth on the table by the window, and began taking plates and glasses, spoons, forks and knives, from the cupboard. Meanwhile two cousins had come in, man and wife, the latter in a blue silk dress, and after them came a rosy young niece and several other relatives. Each guest made a sign of the cross and a slight genuflection before the ikon near the door. Then each was introduced to us. The visit of an American created an impression. This was to be no informal affair. A quick vigorous handshake and a bow. Then silence all about the room—till Tarasov in his genial way started the conversation.

The head of the house had now come in, a strong grizzled man in his fifties, with black eyes alert and keen. The dinner was served: a large cold fish, a loaf of black bread, and a saucer filled with fresh caviar; also buns and jam and tea, which all drank from glasses. As the meal went on, they drank glass after glass until their faces glistened. The room grew warm, and we opened the windows for the cool breeze from the river. Through the meal, our smiling hostess kept coming in and out from the kitchen, stopping to listen now and then. The talk at the table had centered little by little around our host, whom Tarasov was drawing out for my especial benefit. Soon the man was giving his point of view on the revolution. The others sat listening stolidly, the men now and then lighting fresh cigarettes. Only by a low chuckle or a

---

[5] Singer sewing machines, manufactured at a plant near Moscow, had become common throughout Russia, thanks to staggered payment plans and peasant bank loans. By 1917, however, a shortage of needles and thread limited their use.

sudden gleam in their eyes could you see how closely they followed his points. For as foreman of the river gang, he was one of the leading men in the village.

To begin with, he insisted that the new government must be forced to give the peasants more land, and to prove the justice of his claim he went back many years in his life.

"When we pulled down the old hut to build this one," he said, "we found in the attic a pile of receipts for the taxes paid to the government for the land we were given in 1861 (the time of the Emancipation). My grandfather, my father and I have paid so many taxes for our five desiatinas (twelve acres) here, that the land could be quite covered with the money that we gave for it. My father and I were made to pay thirty-six rubles every year, and to get that money in the old days cost us plenty of sweat and blood.

"There was scarcely a week in all the year that we were not working hard. All through the summer we worked on the farm. From October until May, we fished and logged on the river. And when there was no other work to do, we used to drag up sunken logs from the river bottom. That was a slow, hard job. On a freezing winter morning we would take two boats out on the ice. With our axes we would chop through the ice and make a space as big as this hut. Into this space we would shove the two boats and fill them with water. Then with spiked poles we would feel for the logs on the bottom twenty feet below. We would drive four poles into a log and fasten the poles by chains to the boats. Then we would bail the water out, and the boats would rise because they must—as you might say, by the will of God. And as they rose, with the spiked poles they would pull the log loose from the mud below. It took nearly a day to get one log, and for this we received between one and two rubles.

"Again we would gather the firewood that drifted down from barges broken up in the cataracts. We hired out as watchmen, too, to guard the logs on the riverside. Before the railroad was laid down, my father used to drive travelers in a sledge one hundred versts (sixty-five miles) to Petrograd, and when he came back from such a long journey, he would look like Grandfather Frost. So we labored; so we saved. It was a heavy life. As soon as the ice broke up in the spring, we were always either fishing or working this small farm of ours. When I married I was a lucky man, for my wife was a fine helper. Her hands have been like gold to me. She planted the vegetable garden here; she raised chickens and pigs, and all the time she made my old man and me comfortable. Such cooking! You can taste for yourself. And you see how clean she keeps the hut.

"But this is what I want to say. I say this land is all our own, and that now we ought to have still more, because since 1861 we have paid the government many times its value. The Czar is our debtor, so now I claim it is quite right and legal for us peasants to take more land for ourselves. Nor will we ask for it as alms. We will take first the lands of the Crown and then the private owners' estates. The trouble will come in dividing it up. How that will be done, I do not know. It must be managed in such a way so as not to stop the farming—for God knows we need all the grain we can raise.

"I don't believe that the cities will be able to help us in this, for they know nothing of our real needs and they work all kinds of foolish tricks. Just to give you one case—they move forward the hands of the clock, and they call it 'daylight saving.' How does this 'daylight saving' work? I used to get up in the morning at five. All right, I get up at the same time still, except that by the clock it is six. For the lazy people in towns, the clock may tell them how to live, but for us who already use all the light that the sun can give, what a childish trick this is!

"In the towns they complain that our wood contractors charge too much for firewood. But how can they expect us to sell it at a lower price, when here in the stores we have to pay such enormous prices for everything that comes to us from the city? The towns will not give us what we need. We are afraid to mow fast in the fields, for we know that if we should break our scythes, there are no others to be had. And we have to mow, or we shall starve. Yet now they say in the cities that we should sell at prices fixed by the new government. But we will not sell at *any* price! They won't get any grain from us, so long as things go on like this![6]

"Just take a trip to Petrograd. Go to any railroad siding there and you will see perfect hills of scrap iron. Why can't they melt it up again and put it to use? Soon we shall have no axles left, no tires for our wagon wheels, no chains for the logs, no plows for the fields, no horseshoes for our horses! But still they do nothing! The blind fools! The trouble with those people is that they think all the best things are made in the cities. It is not so. Here we grow the flax and grain; here we raise the meat they eat, and the wool to keep them warm; we cut trees to build their houses and firewood to heat their stoves. They could not even cook without us! Other country districts turn out the coal and iron ore. All the real things in Russia are done in the villages. What kind of crops do they raise in the towns? Only Grand-Dukes, Bolsheviks and drunkards! I tell you it would be possible to have a whole country without any cities—only small towns and villages, all joined together by railroads. And I am sure we should do very well. The cities we do not need at all. The cities make people think like men who have fallen sick and are lying in bed with a fever. Only on farms or deep in the forest or out on the river while you fish, can you think a thing out clearly. For there your life goes quietly, and you learn only what is worth while.

"This whole revolution was manufactured in the towns, and it is as flimsy as other town productions. Look how shallow it runs. They say, 'This is a democracy. We speak for all the people.' But how can they claim to speak for us when we have never heard of them? What right have they to speak in our names and say that the peasants want this and that, when we have not yet opened our mouths? That is dam-

---

[6] At least part of the problem was that there was plenty of food in the country, since no exports were possible, but transportation was breaking down and costs escalating.

nable trickery! Between them and us there is the same gap as between a man who drives a sledge and another man who rides on a train. The first one has plenty of time to think, out under the sun or the stars at night; the second is rushed along in the train and chatters like a babbling fool, and meanwhile thinks nothing clear at all, except what rotten tobacco the man next to him is smoking.

"That is how they are in the towns. They want to change Russia in a day. What idiots! It cannot be done. If I have a piece of virgin soil to turn into arable land, first I shall have to plow it well, then harrow it and seed it down, and by the time I have produced the right rotation of crops on that field, I will have spent perhaps five years—and all for the simple matter of a few desiatinas of soil. But here these people in cities are proclaiming such reforms as have never been tried throughout the world—and yet they try to rush them through! Once I read a big brown book that told about the life of the world; and in the first chapter I read to my wife that the seven days of creation, which the Bible tells about, were really a matter of millions of years, but that a million years and a day are all the same to the great God. Are these town people gods that they will rebuild the whole world in a day, and the minds and habits of all people on it?

"They have begun from the wrong end. If they had been wise, at the very start, as soon as they had dethroned the Czar, they would have brought iron discipline into the Russian army, both at the front and at the rear; and in the towns they would have said to all the loafers, 'You must work!'

"What armies of idlers are in the towns. I shouldn't wonder if four-fifths of the people in Petrograd simply loafed, all of them waiting for Russia to starve, while out here every pair of hands could be used at a big profit. I am sure that by next March, Petrograd will have nothing to eat. Then swarms of these loafers will come to us. And what shall we do? For half of them are soldiers, and our peasant pitchforks are no good against their rifles. Perhaps the outcome of it will be that we shall be forced to feed these beasts and starve ourselves—all because they are loafing now!"

The peasant broke off with an anxious scowl and his nephew, the young ensign, said in a low, quiet tone, "Why should you let them take your grain? Why not fight for it like men? I can raise a company here myself that will stand against that city crowd. They are nothing but garrison troops who have never seen a gun pointed their way. If you let them have your wheat and rye, they will sell it all to Germany. The best thing is to let them starve, until they listen to reason and lick the army into shape. All the officers I know, and a good many soldiers, too, would be glad to see the death penalty back. A few thousand fellows hanged and shot would save perhaps millions of lives later on. As it is, we are getting ready to let the German armies in."

He turned to Tarasov and added, in his toneless even voice: "There are crowds of deserters everywhere hiding in the villages. And we can't arrest them, because the peasants say, 'What is the use? Why send these boys to Petrograd to sit on park benches and loaf with the rest?'"

Watching his gaunt, quiet face, I thought what a boy he was himself. A veteran at twenty-two, he had had three years of war, had been in the Brusilov drive, that vast resistless rush of men by millions for two hundred miles, day and night with fearful losses, far down into Hungary. What black hideous nightmares, what prodigious panoramas he had seen. Then I heard him saying softly,

"It is hard to tell what will happen before all this has come to an end. But some of us will keep waiting until we see a real chance for an army. It may be a year—it may be two. But we are waiting, men like me, all over Russia. You will see. We don't want the Kaiser in place of the Czar. We want to be rid of both of them."

## 4

As we were about to leave, another visitor arrived, a genial giant of a man who greeted Tarasov like an old friend. Tall, erect and muscular, he had handsome, regular features, a blond mustache and bushy hair. He wore a light gray summer suit, as a man in the city might have dressed, and his manner was easy and assured. He had been a peasant boy, but now he was part owner of a saw-mill down the river. Tarasov had helped him, two years before, to install a turbine wheel, and now as they talked about the mill, he asked us to come and see him soon.

We went to his place on the following day. It was about a mile away, on the opposite bank of the river. A small, ragged girl about eight years old rowed us across in a battered dory, and indignantly declined my offer to help her with the oars. On the other side we tramped along till we came to a large village of some forty or fifty huts in a long row on the riverbank. This village had come into life as an adjunct to the saw-mill, which at the outbreak of the war had employed two hundred hands. The mill was a huge, long building, with mounds of shavings and sawdust about. We found it cool and dim inside, a cavernous place where the air was full of the shrieks of the saws as they tore through the logs: Some forty peasants were working there. Suddenly a whistle blew, and at once all stopped their work. It was five o'clock. Soon we had the place to ourselves, and while we waited for his friend, Tarasov told me about him.

"This chap is typical," he said, "of tens of thousands of small millers, contractors, country storekeepers and the like, who long before the revolution were coming to be a class by themselves. Although a small minority, they are the men of personal force in their towns or villages, and they will have to be reckoned with in the building of the new Russia. Moreover, as these fellows force their way up from the bottom, they are met by men like me from the top, small landowners, country gentlemen, who are far more democratic than the great landed proprietors, and want a free Russia on practical lines. Take my case. As you have seen, I am welcomed everywhere we go—

most of all by this type of peasant. He and I understand each other like brothers, for our interests are the same. Besides, there has been marriage between us. Though my mother was of noble birth, my father was of peasant stock. And the oldest daughter of my friend the mill-owner here was married last year to the son of the landowner over across the river. He was an officer in the Guards.

"And yet, thirty years ago, this girl's father was a ragged boy who with his older brother fed the hogs for a landowner nearby. The two boys were ambitious and worked hard. This one used to come at night to my father's house to borrow books. He was then sixteen. I was at that time just finishing the gymnasium (high school) in the district town, to prepare for the university. And this chap and I became good friends. I found that the books which appealed to him were always those on mechanics. He had little spare time, most of the year, for he got up at five in the morning, and was busy until night. Still, when I say 'busy' I mean it in the Russian way. In a Russian busy day there are plenty of times outdoors or within when a boy or a man can talk or read. You Yankees smile at us for that just as you are smiling now, and just as I have seen you smile when we went to busy offices in Petrograd in the afternoons and found them drinking tea there."

"For an hour or two," I put in.

"Exactly," said Tarasov, "while Yankees always rush along. But I think it would do both of us good if you Americans stopped at times to think what you are doing, and we Russians tried a little more to do what we are thinking."

I still smiled at my Russian friend. I liked Tarasov. Little by little we had come to understand each other well.

"Go on with your yarn about the two brothers."

"Well," he continued, "while one studied books on mechanics and made toy sawmills and other machines, the older brother stuck so hard to the work on his master's estate that soon he was made manager there; and so in six or seven years they had saved up about eight hundred rubles between them. Then they built a little mill, not half the size of this one, and got a few small timber contracts. They had a hard time for the next five years, but after that, they were on their feet, and now their business has so grown that this large village has sprung up along the riverbank, simply to house their workingmen. So much for the peasant who had fought his way well up in life before the revolution. How is he going to take it now?"

Juvenale Ivanovich was going on to speak of this when the mill owner himself came in. Tall, powerful and self-assured, he seemed to be the sort of man who could wield a deal of influence. At present, there could be no mistake about his hostility toward a part at least of the revolution. In a quiet, smiling way, he told how several years ago he had worked his men in two shifts of twelve hours each. Later, he said, he had found it paid better to increase his force and work three eight-hour shifts in the mill, because in that way he increased the pace. But since the revolution, the men had gone crazy, he declared.

"They said, 'Now we are all free men, and no free men will work at night.' I told them that I quite agreed. 'So long as you feel as free as that, I will let two-thirds of you go,' I said, 'and work only one shift of eight hours here.'" He looked around the dim shadowy place, left idle for the present, but it did not seem to bother him. "We shall go on," he said, "in time. Good wages and three eight-hour shifts—that is a combination that no revolution can stop for long. Come and have a look at my machines."

As he took us through the mill and talked of the big saws and lathes, there was something deep as youth itself in his absorption in these things. Plainly they were new to him still. His expanding life had just begun, and the war and the revolution were only interruptions. He gave me the feeling I'd had before in this quiet country neighborhood, a feeling of the power of the daily job and life, of habit and regular routine, over the decisions of men. Such places and such men as this, scattered all through Russia, would exert a steady pressure, slowly increasing month by month. Against it the Bolsheviks would storm, but the new free nation that emerged would not be what they had seen in their dreams.

In the tool shop of the mill, the owner showed us his two sons, a boy of six and another of twelve. They made me think at once of their father, for together they were engrossed at a lathe, turning out a new axle for their small wagon, to which they were going to harness their dog.

"It's better than a school for them," their father said, as we went away. "They are here for hours every day."

He took us to his home nearby, a white frame house two stories high. Plainly we were expected there, for a bouncing "hired girl" eagerly opened the door for us, and while we waited in the front room we could hear excited voices upstairs. I was interested to see this home of the people who had been peasants only a few years before. The room was papered in blue and gold. There was a great blue stove of tile rising to the ceiling, and a baby grand piano on which stood a large gramophone with a horn of vivid green. Some fifty discs were piled nearby. The windows had lace curtains; in each was a geranium plant. On the table there was an enormous album of purple plush, in which had been pasted hundreds of postcards scribbled by friends all over Russia. Some were from soldiers and officers down along the Russian front, including the young lieutenant who had married the oldest daughter here. She was not at home at present, but her mother and the younger daughter soon came down to see us. Ushered into the dining-room, we sat about the table and were served with tea, black bread and jam.

"Black bread is solid food," said the mother. "White bread is nothing but trimmings," she added, with good-natured scorn. She was an enormous woman, weighing a full two hundred pounds. In her plain black dress she sat at the table, talking little but watching closely to see that each one of us ate enough. The moment I had drunk my tea, she insisted on filling my glass again. To drink less than four or five glasses was an insult to the hostess. She seemed to have little interest in anything outside her house and the flower and vegetable garden outside, which she attended to herself.

Meanwhile, the daughter, a slim brunette of about sixteen who had donned in our honor a blue silk waist, was eagerly telling Tarasov about the winter just gone by. She had nothing to say of the revolution; she had apparently missed all that. For her there had been something vastly more engrossing—her first year in boarding school. She talked gayly of the things she had learned and of all the fun she had had in that school in the district town. There she had gone each Monday morning and had come home on Saturday night. She told of the new friends she had made and the plays in which she had taken part; she spoke of the new dances come all the way from America. As I watched her, I wondered whether she, too, would marry an officer of the Guards.

Would there be any Guards? What was coming in Russia? Certainly such people as these would oppose any extreme leveling down. Even the good-natured mother spoke with a sharp bitterness against the river hooligans who had tried to start riots here—"with their lies and their crazy nonsense about robbing honest people like us of what we have spent our lives to get!"

Soon a brisk little woman came in and was hospitably received. She was a charity worker who had been sent out from Petrograd with some forty orphan children. Through the aid of our hostess, she had rented for next to nothing a large empty house nearby, and there she was giving the children a summer in the country. The stout peasant mother was sympathetic toward this work.

"When people like us get up in the world we expect to help the poor," she said. There was a placid pride in her eyes.

## 5

We left these brand new bourgeois, with their vigor and zest in life and their smiling self-reliance, and walked off down the riverbank past long straggling rows of log huts and hovels, the homes of their workingmen. These people, too, had been peasants only a few years before; but now the men were mill hands. Here among the peasants themselves had risen the clash of interest between employer and employed. I wondered what would come of it? I liked this owner of the mill, with his quiet passion for work and his immense vitality; I liked his wife and their two small boys and their girl, with her fresh animation. But I was growing hungry for a glimpse of the *other* people.

"Let's see a few of these hooligans," I proposed to Tarasov. "You have shown me the respectable lot—and they're all very fine—but they're not enough. They all agree too nicely with your own outlook on life, and your own pet cure and salvation for Russia."

Tarasov walked in silence. His expression had grown grim.

"All right," he said. "I shall prove to you that I can be a good fellow, too, even with the hooligans. My father used to paint them, and I used to help by mixing among them to find models for his brush."

In the dusk, which was fast deepening, we tramped along the riverbank. Presently from down by the water we heard a gay hubbub of voices, sudden laughter now and then; and coming around the corner of an old log stable, we saw a score of men and boys, their faces lighted in the dark by a large bonfire there, with a couple of black iron pots swinging slowly over the flames. Close by the door of the stable was a short stocky man with black hair, who was busy with an ax and knife cutting up the carcass of a cow. He claimed that they had bought it from a peasant up the river. As he tossed the great chunks of meat into a barrel beside him, and sprinkled in coarse salt from a bag, he explained that they were raft men who had put in to camp for the night. Soon the crowd caught sight of us and called to us to come and sit down.

So we had another tea party, but there was nothing bourgeois here! This spot had often been used before by such gangs for a bivouac. A huge log served as a table, and on logs on either side sat two rows of men and boys hungrily devouring enormous chunks of black bread, and drinking from their dirty tin cups strong tea and a meat soup they had made. There were two small pails of blackberries into which each dipped his hand. They were a noisy rollicking crowd.

"Where are you from?" Tarasov asked.

"Most of us from Novgorod," cried a short towheaded chap, with a bullet head and wide square jaws. "Where the devil else could we have come from? See what hooligans we are. Only in Novgorod, brother, does God make such specimens!"

"That's a lie," said a tough red-headed boy, who looked about fifteen years old. His mouth was quite full at the moment; with an effort he gulped down his food. "We come from all over," he declared. "I come myself from just down the river. God only knows where I shall end. Before I get through I will make every river in Holy Russia give me a ride. That's the fellow I am!"

Then a thin, stoop-shouldered, gaunt-looking man, with a ghost of a twinkle in his eye, said solemnly to Tarasov:

"It was sad news for us, Barin, when our beloved little Czar was kicked off his golden throne. Sorrow weighed down upon our souls to such a degree that we left our raft and climbed far up a wooded hill to a holy monastery there, which had the same name as our Czar. Saint Nicholas was its patron saint. And so, to the glory of Nick the Saint and of Little Nick the Czar, we went in and took the holy relics, stuff all made of gold and silver jewels stuck in everywhere. And we piled them all upon our raft, so that none of those sinful Bolsheviks should get a chance to rob the good God. When we came near to Petrograd, we hid them all in a little wood. And there, when it had been arranged, we sold them one night to three Petrograd Jews. Then we made them kneel on the ground and beg us not to cut their throats. We let them load the holy stuff into an old automobile—and off they went, while we sang them a song."

"These Bolsheviks," growled a man with a square head and a short heavy beard already half gray. "Bolsheviks, Bolsheviks—how they shout about being free men. What do they know about being free? They know nothing but books, they sit indoors and scribble and read and talk like clerks—and they are so busy making us free that they have no time to be free themselves! Let them come and find what freedom is! We'll show 'em!"

There was a chorus of cries.

"Turn their stomachs inside out," declared the tough red-headed boy. "Then take those stomachs in a pile down to the river and scrub them well—and give them back to the little men, and say, 'Now, brothers, see how good it feels to be free of all your thinking!'"

One of the youngsters started a song, and the rest came in on the refrain—to the glory of their wandering life. Here indeed were Ishmaelites, abhorred by respectable villagers. There were perhaps a million such men on the long winding rivers of Russia, from Archangel to the Volga and far down to Astrakhan.[7] Their ranks were recruited constantly from villages along the way; for the river called, and the peasant boys strolled into the bivouacs at night, and soon they joined the wanderers; working and sleeping on their rafts, stopping now and then to buy or steal the meat and other provisions they needed. They earned good wages, and some of them sent money home to their families, but most had sprees in the larger towns—or at least they did in the old vodka days.[8]

Tarasov, as we walked away, told of other wanderers—of the armies of labor that roamed about from one big job to another, on railroads, bridges, dams, canals; and of the traveling blacksmiths and tailors and shoemakers who made a semi-hobo class. I stopped to look back on the firelight and the small black figures of men and boys; I listened to their singing, their voices and their laughter, and to the sweet low voice of the river murmuring close by my side. I thought of the thousands of bivouacs along the rivers of the land that were burning that night and would still burn in the many nights ahead. They would be multiplied tenfold. For as the armies disbanded, innumerable recruits would come to join these wandering hooligans. I wondered what part they would play in the tumultuous months ahead. The Great Revolution had so many parts, so many jarring factors. I recalled the radical workingmen whom I had seen in the cities, the thrifty prosperous peasants that my friend had shown me here, and the many more in Russia who lived in darkest poverty—White Russians and Ukrainians, Tatars, Finns, Caucasians. And I wondered what these elements, dashing one upon

---

[7] This is the origin of the famed "Volga boatmen."

[8] Reference here is to the decree on prohibition at the beginning of the war.

the other, would make of it all before they got through. The future of Great Russia was wrapped in mysterious shadows.

Suddenly from up the river a watchman who was guarding the logs sent out his long and mournful cry. It was taken up from the opposite bank; it was echoed by a voice down stream, then by another farther down, and so traveled away in the heavy night.

**Figure 1.** "The Dark People"

**Figure 2.** Market Day

**Figure 3.** Peasant Veterinary Doctors

# Chapter III

## 1

What's a village without a "general store"? The hamlets in this neighborhood were mere clusters of log huts, without a shop of any kind; but across the river, about a mile from the home of my friend, was a much larger village where centered the district's social life.

Our first visit there I remember well. From our side of the river we ferried across in a leaky old boat which we rowed ourselves. The ferryman kept half a dozen such dories moored at a rude little pier by his hut. We paid him our fare of a few kopecks each, and rowing across to the village wharf we climbed up the riverbank and so came to the village street. It was very wide and very short, and was covered deep with limestone dust. Most of the houses were log affairs, one and a half or two stories high. We went first into the post-office, a large bare room with a high counter which was glass enclosed at one end. The Czar's picture had been torn from the wall, and in its place hung a big red poster of a Russian soldier fighting. Underneath were the words, "Fight till Victory." This was one of the many appeals for the new Russian Liberty Loan, sent out to all the villages by the Kerensky Government. Here, the glum postmaster told us, it had met with little response.

"There have been so many loans," he said. "The peasants are sick of paying, paying. All their lives they have done nothing else. They want a rest from taxes now."

He turned back to a ledger in which he was writing. Plainly he did not care to talk. So we left him, went down to the street and entered the general store nearby. It was full of grocery odors. There were a few tin canisters of tea and other groceries, and boxes of potatoes, tomatoes, beans and cucumbers. In the one glass showcase was a very meager array of thread and pins and needles, and a few other odds and ends, including a little candy and packages of cigarettes. The woman in charge did not seem to be worried over the fact that her shelves were so bare. She had still a few bales of calico prints. These, she said, were the last of her stock, which she had procured two months ago when she went to Petrograd.

"I bought all I could lay my hands on," she said, "for I saw what was coming. Now I can get hardly anything more. But why worry?" she added, with a shrug. "One has to change one's ways, that is all." And she pointed up to the big brown beams under her low ceiling. From two of them hung coarse woolen mits of all sizes, some white and others brown. "The peasants spun that wool themselves," she continued quietly. "I have two or three women friends among them, and we are planning to do a good deal of this work when the winter comes. When the government agents arrive, we hide the few sheep that are left in the woods. For I say if the cities can give us nothing, we will at least keep what is ours. With that we shall manage to get along until life is better in Russia."

A stout peasant woman came in just then, with a sack of potatoes in one hand and in the other a package of wool. The wool and potatoes were carefully weighed, and there was much discussion. The storekeeper took a small ax from the wall, and going to a corner where stood a huge block of sugar about two feet high, she eyed it for a moment and then cautiously chipped off a chunk. This she weighed and chipped again. What was left she wrapped in brown paper, and this, together with a small package of tea and a paper of pins and needles, she handed to her customer, in return for the potatoes and wool. No money had passed between them. Just plain old-fashioned barter here.

After the customer had gone, there was an awkward moment. For Tarasov and I were out foraging; we were sorely in need of a loaf of bread, tea, butter, jam and potatoes. We eyed the storekeeper uneasily. Then Tarasov forced a smile.

"Although we have nothing but money," he said, "if you will be so good and kind as to let us have some provisions—"

The woman smiled good-naturedly:

"Juvenale Ivanovich," she replied, "was not your father always doing kind things for my family? Surely I'll take your money now."

And she did—she took a lot of it. But gratefully gathering in the provisions we said good-by and started home.

## 2

On another day we stopped in for lunch at a "tea house" or restaurant which occupied one of the four main corners on the village street. It had a few sleeping rooms above, for the use of post road teamsters. In the dining room, which was far from clean, we found three or four peasants at tables making a meal of tea and bread. The proprietor, a quiet man, had long been a friend of Tarasov's. About fifty years old and of medium size, he was dressed in gray, with a bright blue shirt. He had a scraggy blond mustache, high cheek bones, a strong steady face and one glass eye which gave him rather a stony expression. He took us into his living-room, which was deliciously cool and clean. The walls and low ceiling were plastered in gray; at the windows were white curtains, and a heavily curtained bed stood over in one corner. He spread the small table with a clean cloth, and after serving us luncheon there, he sat down and lit a cigarette.

The talk soon turned to the question of how to get food supplies from the peasants and of how to get goods from the towns. He was one of the local supply committee. The chairman, he informed us, was the former starosta (village elder); the secretary was a young student, the illegitimate son of the midwife; and there were four peasant members besides. The committee had control of the work in thirty-nine villages, including the little hamlets up near Tarasov's farm.

"In each village we have a peasant," he said, "who brings us a report every week of what grain and fodder his neighbors have. But the reports are all the same. The peasants will not give up their grain until they can get real goods in trade, and as yet, we can get so few goods from the towns that we cannot persuade the peasants to take their grain out of their barns.

"The only hope that I can see is in our Cooperative here. Our cooperative store has still quite a stock of goods, and the steadier peasants all belong. We have eighteen hundred members now. Each paid five rubles to buy a share. There were six thousand purchasers last year, and because we charge higher prices to outsiders than to members, so many more peasants wish to join that we are almost ready to announce a second issue of stock. Last year the daily turnover was twenty-five hundred rubles.

"Of course, our progress has been blocked by the war and the revolution. Goods have gone up to ruinous rates. Already we are nearly out of horseshoes, axes, harrows, plows. Last spring we had not plows enough to do the needed plowing, and that is why our crop is short. There is not enough rye in the district to take us through the winter, let alone to feed the towns. And so the town people will starve for awhile—and sooner or later, I suppose, they will finish with their wrangling, start their mills and factories, and turn out the plows and tools we need.

"Our Cooperative is even now preparing for that time ahead. We are not only growing here but we are getting in closer touch with other societies like ours. We have already joined the Union of Cooperatives. In every province in Russia there is such a Union, and the Unions get big credits from the People's Bank in Moscow, which is like a mother of them all. The Unions have altogether more than thirteen million members now. So we are no small affair. We are a power in Russia today, and even bad as things may be, our mother Bank in Moscow is already planning to send relief. Through credits advanced to us from that Bank, our Union in this province is building some big flour mills, in order to keep the whole grain business in our hands. More and more we peasants will control the food supplies of the country.

"The revolution keeps breaking in, for the hooligans are always trying to make our peasants riot here. At the start, the peasants chose me as head of our militia police. I took as my assistant the man who keeps the coöperative store, and from the revolutionary committee of the district we got two swords and two revolvers—not very much for an army—but we managed to keep the peace until about three weeks ago, when a mob of peasants and hooligans tried to break into the store. We stood in front and kept them off—while they buzzed and talked and shouted.

"'This is a very bad business,' we told them. 'You'd better go home and keep the peace.' And most of the older peasants went home. But the younger ones decided to raid the house of your neighbor, Prince C. As you will remember, some years ago, by order of the government the Prince had been appointed the honorary chairman and treasurer of the Cooperative. And last winter, when the time came to pay to us a dividend, the Prince had insisted on using the money instead to build here a People's House with a moving picture show. The peasants had been enraged at the scheme because it was done without their consent. So now they decided to search his house and go through his account books. There were nearly six hundred there in the street, all shouting and working themselves up. It was an ugly business. I tried to talk sense into them and show them how crazy was their plan.

"'What can you do,' I shouted, 'if you all rush into the Prince's house? Suppose you get his papers. How can you understand them? Brothers, you must all wait here and let the storekeeper and me go up and talk this out with the Prince. For we are used to such things as accounts, and we will bring you back the truth.'

"But one young peasant shouted at me, 'You fellows know *too much* of accounts! You are merchants! We want none of your tricks! Now it is revolution and we will do these things ourselves!'

"So off they rushed like a herd of young bulls. But it took a long time to get them all into boats and across the river, and after that, when they had climbed the long hill and walked a mile in the rain, by the time the first ones reached the place, they were cooled off and they waited around. At last, when the others had come up, they broke into the house and went through his rooms till they found his desk, and from this they took out all the papers. They brought them back to the village, and here all night they shouted and argued and tried to make something out of it all. But the columns of figures in those accounts were as mysterious to them as the spells of the village sorcerer. By morning these fine revolutionists had their tongues hanging out of their mouths. They slept all day, and that was the end of the only riot we have had here.

"But there is always danger still from these chaps, and the soldiers from the towns are always looking for trouble. The troops who come home from the front on leave are different, they are a steady crowd—but these fellows who have been loafing in towns are nothing but bums and robbers.

"Last week, three soldiers came into my tea-room. Two of them were older men, a fairly steady looking pair, but one was a thin youngster and he had uneasy eyes. I knew him at once for a barracks bum. He came into my place with his cap on. He gave me no 'Good morning.' Just threw his money on the table.

"'Tea,' he said. I took no notice. A woman came in, and I served her first. He looked up and scowled at her. Then I brought tea and bread and eggs to the two older soldiers. The youngster scowled again and asked, 'Don't you understand what that means?' He pointed to his money.

"'Of course I don't,' I answered. He jumped up and his face got red.

"'Now I'll give you a lesson!' he cried. But I said,

"'I will do it first. And the lesson you need is this. When you enter a tea-room, take off the cap from your empty head, and don't throw down your money as though you owned me like a slave. You think that you can make me feel that you are a brave soldier and I am only a muzhik. But I know you are only a loafer, my friend. All day long in Petrograd, you walk about eating sunflower seeds and spitting them out. Instead of defending your country, you have spit all over it.'

"The fellow kept glaring at me. 'You don't mean to give me tea?' he demanded.

"'Of course not,' I answered him. 'Go back to Petrograd, my boy, and tell your young friends how to behave. If you'll stop attacking sunflowers and go and kill a few Germans instead, you may grow up to be a man.'

"The lad looked at his older comrades for help, but they grinned at him and chuckled, because they knew that I was right. So he had to sneak out of the tea-house."

Our host's glass eye was solemn enough, but the other one twinkled as he talked. Now he lit a fresh cigarette and went on in a more serious tone:

"The trouble is that men like me have no guns behind us, and so it is hard to keep order. The new government in Petrograd does not give us any support. They allow only two militia men here to keep order in thirty-nine villages. We should have at least fifty armed men. We should have telephones, besides, to every little village, and a policeman in each one, and we should have two or three automobiles for bringing them all together at once to any spot where they are needed. As it is, the young river hooligans steal horses and cattle—and what can we do? Besides, if we had a telephone, when a fire broke out in a village they could lend a call for help. As it is, if a village starts to burn, there is nothing to do but pray to God.

"Three months ago, all the militia heads like me were told to come to B— (the chief city of the province) and listen to a fine address by the president of the Zemstvo [local assembly] there, who would tell us poor peasants what to do. So we gathered from all over the province, and one after another we came into the big hall—a very handsome place where the old Zemstvo used to meet. Our meeting had been called at four. We looked at the clock, the hour had come, but there was no sign of a meeting. Only some girl typewriters and a few young clerks to be seen. No one paid any attention to us, nor did they answer our questions. At last I called out, 'We had better go home.' At that a clerk designed to give us the news that the president would be with us soon. So we waited about an hour more. Then another clerk came in and said, 'The president begs me to bring you excuses. Unfortunately he is busy and cannot spare time for you today. But his assistant will speak to you.'

"In came a young assistant, and in a voice as sweet as a woman's he told us things that each of us had known since we were little brats, about being good and sensible.

In our villages, he said, we must talk in a quiet sensible way to all troublemakers, and ask them to be patient, and so prevent all riots and mobs. I got sick of his talk.

"'Now then, fellow,' I called out, 'for Christ's sake tell us something real. What are my duties and what are my powers as head of militia? There is no judge in my neighborhood now. Am I to be judge? Some peasants have come with their quarrels and asked me to judge them. Shall I do it or shall I not? I did not know, so I did it. I judged their cases as best I could.'

"Then the other sixty militia heads began to speak up, one by one, and to say that they had done the same. And we asked the young assistant whether it was legal. But he confessed he did not know. He went to get the president, and that great official now deigned to come in. He had a big belly and fat wrists; as he walked, he had to carry four chins. He was a well-fed gentleman. Gold spectacles were in his hand. He looked with amusement at us and said:

"'Oh, that's all right, fellows. Just do your best.' He walked out of the hall. And that's all the practical information we ever got out of the town! We came home thanking God and the Saints that we had been born in villages!

"Since then we have settled things for ourselves. And we have been supported by all the more sensible peasants here. Quietly we are planning things out. We have made up our minds we must get more land and also better farm machines. But in Petrograd they only talk, and God knows what the result will be. For the peasants are getting so sick of it all. It is hard to hold the young ones in. Soon they may join the hooligans and the barracks soldiers in the towns, and then with the Bolsheviks they may smash the government. And all because this government will not stop its empty talk and give us what the peasants need! This fellow Kerensky, they tell me, is a well-meaning honest man, and a wonderful speaker, too. When he speaks, he lifts you into the clouds. But the clouds are a very foggy place from which to settle the question of land.

"In the villages," he concluded, "we at least have done our part. I will take you to our Cooperative now and show you how the peasants have organized to buy machines and all the other supplies we need, as soon as the cities can get them. We have done it quietly. No talk or gentleman's plans in books, but a thing that has grown like a crop of rye, right out of the needs of the people themselves. And I tell you this is the crowd that any free, sensible government in Russia must build on. You will see."

# 3

He took us up a side street, and crossing by an old stone bridge a creek that ran into the river under the brow of a rocky cliff, we came to a group of three or four small

## CHAPTER III

brick buildings. High above were the half-ruined walls and turrets of a monastery, one of the ancient fortresses used by the Czars of olden times to repel invaders from the West. Down here was a modern invader, and one more certain to supplant the old autocratic rule—a real community center, owned and run by the people themselves, part of a vast and intricate system of such centers all over the land, that was already affecting the lives of thirteen million families.

We entered first the low brick building which was used as the general store. Five or six peasant women and girls were gossiping there in a leisurely way and looking over some calico prints and ribbons, two small babies' caps, a blanket, several bottles of "pain killer" and various kinds of groceries. It was a kind of a mothers' club. Behind the store was a row of log sheds for the more bulky articles. Here were sacks of seeds of all kinds, seeds imported from the South by agricultural experts employed by the Cooperative Union of the Province as a part of their campaign to promote modern farming. There were bags of fertilizer and some barrels of cement. There were a few farming implements, too, a small harrow and two plows. Nearby, in a larger building was a little farmers' bank where, if a peasant's assets were good, he could get cash at five per cent, and three months' credit on goods in the store. A rear room was being used by the local food supply committee, and also as headquarters of the new town council. The Cooperative had seized the chance to gather in unto itself the revolutionist government here and steady its activities.

On the walls of a room adjoining were charts and pictures showing improved agricultural methods and demonstrating the rich results. In crude and vivid chromos were shown fields of oats and wheat and rye, first under the old cultivation with the resulting meager crops, and then with the new methods producing double or treble the yield. The same was shown of potatoes, peas and beans, tomatoes, cabbages and apples. The breeding, housing and feeding of horses, cattle, pigs and sheep was dealt with on another wall. There were pictures of hot houses, too, and of farm machinery, including one of a huge plow, in early spring, clearing off the snow from a field.

The largest chromo of them all displayed a peasant family before and after joining the Cooperative Society. They were shown at first in squalor and filth in front of a tumbled-down old hut; the women and children, the horse, the cow and even the pig looking puny and half-starved to death. But then behold a miracle! A large new house, a stable and barn, a new plow and harrow, two stout horses and two cows, and a pig fairly beaming with content—while the peasant, his wife and children, all ruddy with health and in brand-new clothes, smiled on their new environment. "We Have Joined the Peasants' Cooperative!" Over this picture was draped a red flag.

## 4

The third building was a hospital. Built by the Cooperative some three years before the war, on the ground floor there had been a dispensary and clinic for mothers and children, run by a woman doctor sent out from Petrograd by a mothers' aid society. The hospital was empty now, for in the second year of the war the government had taken it for the care of wounded soldiers, and so the mothers and children had been left to shift for themselves. But the wounded had all left, and having thoroughly cleaned the place, the Cooperative was looking about for another doctor and a nurse, to continue the work as before.

Meanwhile, on the second floor, the local midwife had been installed. She used two rooms for her living quarters, and the other two, she said, were for serious maternity cases. Employed by the Cooperative to look after the wives of its members, she charged four rubles for each case, which at that time was equivalent to a dollar in our money. If the patient was a soldier's wife, the charge was reduced one half. The midwife was a genial bright little woman of middle age, with quick vigorous movements and a humorous turned-up nose, in striking contrast to her voice, which was a deep, sweet contralto. In her small sunny room there were plants in the windows, gay curtains and pictures all about. After serving us tea, preserved cherries and bread, she brought out her cigarettes, and with a contented sigh she settled down for a good Russian talk.

Although herself a peasant who had always lived in this neighborhood, her mind seemed roving over the world. She had read little, apparently; I saw but two books in her living-room, and both of them dealt with her work. But she asked us eager questions not only about Petrograd but about London, Paris, New York. With her head resting on one hand she would listen intently, and once she broke in with a smile to exclaim, "Just think! A real American here!"

She talked frankly of her work, narrating how in twenty years of attending peasant women, little by little she had picked up new points in her profession. She had never lost a mother, she claimed. The baby? That was different. One could not expect to save every child in such homes as some of these women had. They got along as best they could.

"Sometimes. I meet a patient later. 'Well, what of the child?' I ask her. She answers, 'It lived,' or else, 'It died.'" The midwife shrugged her shoulders. "But there are wonderful women here; they are great breeders," she went on. "They will live and thrive where a horse would die." She smiled as she lit a fresh cigarette.

"Well, since the revolution has come, the main difference I see is that the women have been quite changed; now that they are voters. Their husbands used to thrash them—once a week when sober, and more often when they were drunk. But things are very different now."

Here she broke off for a moment to ask if the woman's movement in England had been stopped on account of the war. When she heard the word "suffragette," the midwife laughed delightedly.

"That was the word I heard about! I was trying to remember!" she cried. "Suffragette! Somebody told me that word was French, and means 'little woman voter.' Well, then, let me tell you that there is nothing little about our peasant women here! Now each one on Saturday night shouts at her man when he comes with his stick, 'Just you try to beat me, and watch how I will spit in your face!' That's what the voting has done for her. Besides, they come crowding to all the new meetings and say, 'We must all have our share! In this new land that we take from the barins, women and men must count alike!'"

Her talk was interrupted by the coming of her son, a slim and wiry, tow-headed lad about twenty years old, dressed in a student's uniform. The fact of his illegitimate birth had not been allowed to shadow his life. His mother had sent him away to school, and now on his return to the village he was a recognized leader here. Only three or four old dames looked askance at his mother and himself. With all the rest, apparently, their social status was perfectly good. And this was no uncommon case of Russian village tolerance.

The boy talked eagerly of his work on the food supplies committee, and of how he was trying to hold the younger men in the village in line and keep them from rioting. The way to do it, he explained, was to keep things humming. Fun was a good safety valve. One week they would get up a picnic, the next an amateur play in the school, with plenty of refreshments served. He was starting a peasants' chorus now. The last play in the school house had netted seven hundred rubles, he said, and this money was to be used to buy a new pump and hose line for the village fire brigade. They were planning to give a score of plays during the coming winter months.

"The next play will be given tonight," he informed us, "and the proceeds are to go to the building fund for the new People's House to be built by the Cooperative. The sooner that building is started, the better it will be for the whole revolution here. It will give them what they need—steady work and wages all through the fall and winter. And it will increase our power, too, for we are the ones to give out the jobs. We will give the jobs to the steadier crowd; the work will keep them together, and little by little we'll arm them all. Then we can control the whole neighborhood."

"In the meantime," said his mother, smiling at him good-naturedly, "you had better arm your stomach, my boy."

Hungrily he helped himself to a glass of tea, and bread and cherries. He kept on talking all the while of what they would do in the People's House. He pointed out of the window to the vacant lot nearby, where the foundations were already laid.

"As soon as we build the first floor," he said, "we shall turn it into a theater. Give the people a good time and keep them out of trouble! We must start giving dances there. We'll get some fellow from Petrograd to come up and show us the new steps.

We want nothing out of date. Then we will start some lectures, too, and get a cinema machine. Perhaps this American writer will tell his friends when he goes home to send us all the films they can, for it will do our peasants good to see how the American peasants live. Tell him to send us picture books showing the life on those big farms where the cows herd with the buffalo. We cannot read the English, but if there are pictures enough in the books they will be used by the peasant till every page is as dirty as the inside of a stable!" He laughed. "We will put these books in the reading-room, on the second floor of our People's House. We'll get a pile of Russian books, too. But tell him if they do not send us books about America, the Germans will send us wagon loads of books and films and pictures to show how good their country is, and what a kind fellow their Kaiser is! That's the way with those devils!"

The little blue clock on the wall struck five. He jumped up and said that he must be off to help rehearse the company for the play at the school house that night. He urged us to come, and we promised that we would surely be on hand. As we started home, on the village street we were stopped by two pretty girls in white who sat at a table in front of the store, selling tickets for the play. We went on down to the village wharf, and found a crowd of two or three hundred men, women and children gathered there to welcome the brass band of the fire brigade in the district town, which was due to arrive on the steamer soon in order to help at the play that night. The little river steamer was slowly puffing up the stream. As it neared the wharf we saw the band, about a dozen peasant boys, most of them youngsters of fourteen in blue and yellow uniforms. At a signal from their leader, up went their horns, and there burst forth a terrific blaring march. This was greeted by cheers from the crowd, and shouts and peals of laughter. The steamer docked, and the band marched off into the village, with the crowd behind them.

As I turned back toward the river, I saw Tarasov talking with a rugged little man, lean and wrinkled, elderly, but straight as a post. He was smiling at the crowd with quite evident delight. He had a large mouth, an enormous nose, gray mustache and receding hairy chin. He was tanned brown from an outdoor life. I was struck at once by his vigorous pose and the genial fire in his eyes.

"Half his life he was the school teacher here," Tarasov explained as we turned away. "We shall have a long talk with him—many talks, for his home is very close to mine. What a prophet he was, what a worker! Look at that school house." And my friend pointed up the hill to a large three-story building of logs which dominated the neighborhood. "He worked and begged for over ten years until he got that school house built. I shall show it to you tonight. But now we must be going home."

From the wharf we climbed down into a dory, with a merry looking little priest who was dressed in a blue woolen gown. He, too, was a friend of Tarasov's and asked us to come and visit him soon. While they talked, I sat in the bow of the boat. It was a beautiful sunset. The river rippled quietly. The noise of the band had died away. Here and there on the water in dug-outs were the motionless figures of men and women fishing with nets, and down through this small fishermen fleet came a dory filled with rough-necks. Two or three were soldier deserters; the rest were ragged village youths. Shouting and singing, they rowed along, and disappeared 'round a bend in the river.

Crossing to the opposite bank, we walked a mile to Tarasov's home.

## 5

In the small garden in front of the house we found Tarasov's tenant, the heavy feeble gray old man, sitting wrapped in a blanket. Beside him sat the Finnish girl, reading aloud from a magazine. As we came in at the garden gate, she looked up quickly with a smile and told us that he was better now. There was something bright and appealing about her. Dressed in a white sailor suit, her figure was sturdy as a boy's; she had large arms and shoulders, stocky wrists and strong brown hands. Her flaxen hair was braided tight, coiled 'round her head. Her face was deeply pockmarked or she might have been good looking. She had a small resolute mouth, bright gray eyes and a quick eager smile. I had noticed her often in the past week. Twice I had seen her in the garden with a book and a pad of paper, very rapidly making notes, and from her mother, the cook, I had learned that the girl had finished school and was hoping to enter a woman's college in the fall.

"Let's take her to the play," I suggested to Tarasov now. And he assented promptly.

"But first," he said, "we shall surely take some soap and towels, and go down to the river and have a fine swim!"

He took his safety razor, too, and persuaded me to try it. It was a terrific instrument. Balancing on a huge pine log that kept moving in the current, I mauled and gouged my tortured face—while as close beside me as they could get, crouched two naked peasant boys. The sun had set and the air was chill, but the urchins forgot to put on their shirts, so intent were they in watching the progress of my instrument. I finished and dove into the stream. We splashed and swam about for a time, then dressed and went up again to the house, where the Finnish girl had supper all ready on the table.

She was dressed to go to the play, in a fresh white skirt and sailor blouse. Through the open door to the kitchen, I could see her at the table with the two young daughters of the lazy peasant next door. Their father, who was czar of his hut, had not allowed them to go to school, and so almost every evening they came in here to the kitchen, where for two hours the Finnish girl labored to teach them to read and write. Now we proposed that her two small pupils should go with us to the schoolhouse that night. At once there was intense excitement, but after that came a terrible moment—for it was revealed to us that these children had no decent clothes. Their meager cotton dresses were patched and torn, and far from clean. Their feet were bare. Obstinately, almost in tears, they kept shaking their heads and swallowing hard. They refused to be seen in such clothes at the school. But the Finnish girl soon brought them around. She sent them home for their shoes and stockings, and when they came back she wrapped them in her mother's cloak and her own. So we started down the path.

On the way we kept meeting peasants from the neighboring hamlets, men, women and children, whole families, all dressed up in their Sunday clothes, white frocks and flowered kerchiefs, the girls with ribbons in their hair, giggling and chattering. Our two small companions pressed close to our sides, with their borrowed cloaks wrapped about them tight. They seemed to thank God for the deepening dusk. Softly but quite savagely Tarasov cursed their father.

Presently, from a side path, the old school teacher hove into view, in a light gray suit, with a Panama hat tipped well back with a festive air, while his stout wife in a pearl silk dress and a large red flowered hat ambled cheerfully at his side. On her big wrist was strapped a watch. She had been the only child, I learned, of a shrewd and thrifty peasant, from whom she had inherited about a hundred acres of land and eleven thousand rubles in cash.

At the ferry, quite a crowd was waiting, while boat after boat was filled and pushed off. We took our turn and ferried across, went on through the village and up a long winding road on the hillside. Now it was dark. Above us the great log school house poured light from its three tiers of windows, and as we drew nearer we could hear a merry hubbub there. Suddenly with a discordant crash the band of the fire brigade broke loose. We found them standing on the steps blowing away for dear life. Three small urchins stood in front, cheeks bulging as they strained for wind with a fierce solemn pride in their eyes, while a score of village youngsters stood watching them with envy.

Before the entertainment began, Tarasov showed me through the school. Built only a few years before, the air still bore the fresh smell of the logs, and the walls were as yet unplastered. Enormous beams ran overhead, supporting the high ceilings. There were huge tile stoves, and the rooms were immense with generous windows. There seemed to me to be room enough for twice the number of children that I had seen in the neighborhood.

"Exactly," said Tarasov. "That was the old teacher's plan—to have plenty of room—more than enough. 'They live in cramped little huts,' he would say. 'Here I want it to be immense. Plenty of space and sunshine, air. A place where the soul of a child can expand.' That is the kind of a man he was. He shall tell you all about it himself, his dream of what a school should be."

We went up the crowded stairs to the main hall on the third floor, where a rough stage had been improvised. The benches were already filling, for the play was soon to begin. We paused in an adjoining room before a long refreshment buffet, where a row of smiling village girls were busy serving to customers tea in glasses, homemade cake, candy, sandwiches and tarts. We purchased candy for our guests. They had been awkward and shy until now, but the sweets helped considerably. We hurried back to get a place, for a stout old peasant had appeared, ringing an enormous bell. We seated ourselves on a bench, and over the heads before us we could see the same old man carefully placing a row of lamps as footlights along the front of the stage. He placed a plank before them, to keep the light out of our eyes. Each moment the crowd grew denser. Some fidgety woman had insisted that the big window near us be shut, and the air was becoming very close. I watched the stolid faces around me, and the expectant gleaming eyes. On the bench in front of us was the foreman of the river gang, in whose hut we had had Sunday dinner. He was here with his wife, his niece and her baby, who was fast asleep. Some other families sat together, but more often the girls and boys were herded in groups in corners or sat in giggling whispering rows. In the midst of the crowd, close by me, in his light blue uniform, I saw a Hungarian soldier. He did not look like a prisoner here. There were four or five in the village, I learned, and they were quite free to go about.

Again the big bell jangled. Slowly the curtain rose, with jerks, and revealed a living-room in the house of a small town merchant. It was one of the old Russian classics by Ostrovsky.[1] I could catch the lines only here and there, just barely enough to follow the story, which was one of comedy satire on the petty bourgeois life in a town of Southern Russia. But in deepening surprise I watched these village players and the spell that they were casting. Like most amateurs, they dragged their lines, but it was just this leisurely art, this lack of all impatience for having anything happen, this deep and delighted absorption in the characters themselves, which was creating this atmosphere, holding this peasant audience, of which the players were a part. There would be a tense silence, then a quick laugh.

I thought of a certain village at home, and of a performance of *Uncle Tom's Cabin* I had seen. What a difference here! No little Eves, no Legrees, no floating cakes of ice, no thrills. These Russian peasant players were giving a picture of country life simply and profoundly real—and the audience was satisfied. For a time I lost the drift of the play and sat there in the darkness, watching the rows of faces and those shining motionless eyes. I remembered the war. It seemed far away. So, too, the revolution. I was down in the deep waters of Great Russia's mighty life. And I fell to dreaming for awhile of some tremendous friendship which might still come out of this bloodstained land. I thought of my country and Russia, of how it would be if they were friends. I thought of their villages and ours, at present in such different worlds. But I thought of all we could get from each other...

Now it was eleven o'clock and they had just finished the second act. In the audience not only the babies but many small children were asleep. The older children and

---

[1] Alexander Ostrovsky (1823–86) was one of the most popular Russian playwrights of the nineteenth century.

parents alike seemed determined to stay till the end. But the room was stifling, we were weary, and we decided to start for home.

Outside, on the winding country road, although the sky was filled with clouds there was still a curious dim light, for a Russian summer's night knows little of the darkness. In the village we stopped for a moment at the cooperative store to get some fresh butter and black bread. The little place was silent and dark, for the storekeeper was still at the play, but our bread and butter, stoutly wrapped, had been left high up on a window sill out of the way of hungry dogs. I looked at the foundation of the People's House close by. Soon there would be "movies" here, and I wondered what effect this would have on the school house play we had seen that night.

We went down to the river, climbed into a dory, and I rowed our party across. Out there it was mysterious, fresh and cool but very still. We passed two shadowy figures, a man and a woman in dugouts with a fishing net between them. How far away from Petrograd! I remembered what Tarasov had said about this murmuring water, how it flowed into a large deep lake with such a configuration of currents that it stayed there many years, and then flowed on to Petrograd. I recalled the sluggish city canals under the bridges of the streets where I had heard the rattle of shots from the machine guns. That sluggish water had once been here! How had this village appeared in those days? And when this quiet water which was so softly rippling against the sides of our dory now, should at last reach the city of Petrograd, what would be there? What kind of a city? What changes would have been wrought by then in the Russian nation and throughout the world?

## 6

On the opposite side of the river we started off through the fields toward home. On the way Tarasov remembered that we were out of matches, and he dropped in to borrow some at the home of a peasant friend. It was nearly twelve o'clock, but from a hut just up the road light streamed from two little windows, and I could hear an accordion there and a hubbub of girls' voices. The music stopped in a burst of laughter, the door of the hut was thrown open wide, and a half dozen chattering girls came out and scattered down the road. Slowly their voices died away. Looking over the rolling fields I could see one tiny light twinkling in the distance out of the edge of a shadowy wood, and to my ears across the meadows came a man's voice singing.

Tarasov returned and we started on. The two small girls who walked at my side were as mute and shy as at the start. They had taken off their shoes and stockings while we were coming across the river, and with the borrowed cloaks on their arms they pattered along in their bare feet. Tarasov walked with the Finnish girl, and with the curious talent he had, of always drawing people out by his fresh and genuine interest, he soon had her talking about herself. Though her voice was low it was so clear that walking close behind them, even with my poor Russian, I could get snatches now and then. In speaking of the play that night, good-naturedly she complained of the way they had let the action drag. She spoke like one familiar with the theater's inner life, and Tarasov found that she had worked in a theater in Finland. Now her talking grew so rapid that I could not make out a word—but when we reached home he told me her story while she was starting the samovar.

"She is a wonderful girl," he declared. I yawned and lit a cigarette. I was used to such beginnings, for to this Russian friend of mine nearly every one was wonderful.

"She was born in a town in Finland," he said, "I think she was illegitimate. The mother left her baby with a Lutheran family there and went alone to Petrograd, where she became cook for this old man. The child grew up, and from the time she was eight years old she made up her mind to be a doctor. She worked hard in a Lutheran school, and all went well with her for a time. Then the family with whom she lived became very poor, for the man ran a theater in the town and it was not doing well. He had to cut down his employees, and so this girl, who was ten years old, had to help usher every night. But then came a long secret struggle with her conscience, for in the Lutheran school she attended there was a strict rule forbidding the children ever to enter a theater, because it was a sinful place. She grew nearly sick with the struggle she had. She told no one. It grew worse and worse. At last she confessed to one of her teachers, and when the teacher smiled and told her that it was all right, she said she felt such a wave of relief that she will remember it all her life. That is the kind of a girl she is. Her face—you can see how quiet it is, but there is passion underneath.

"She came to her mother in Petrograd, where this old man ran a canning factory. He was a kindly old gentleman, always helping people. He had a habit of buying new clothes for any man or woman or child whom he saw ragged on the streets. He grew interested in this child, with her strange desire to be a physician. Strange? No, I should not call it that—for the thing is common in our land. It was nearly seventy years ago when Russian girls made their first attack to get into the medical profession. Soon they were clamoring at the doors of the Medical University.[2] They were refused. Women doctors! It was a terrible scandal then! Some of the girls were from wealthy homes, but they left their families, lived in cheap rooms, where they froze and

---

[2] The "young Finn" may have been aware of the ground breaking work of Adelaide Lukanina (also known as Paevskaia) in the 1870s, as she was forced to seek a medical education, first in Zurich, then at the Women's Medical College of Pennsylvania, followed by an internship at the New England Hospital for Women and Children in Boston. A. N. Paevskaia, *God v Amerike: Iz vospominanii zhenshchiny-vracha* [A Year in America: From the Memoirs of a Woman Doctor (St. Petersburg, 1892). *See also* Jeannette Tuve, *The First Russian Women Physicians* (Newtonville, MA: Oriental Research Partners, 1984).

starved, reading medical books. Quite a few of them killed themselves. In the end the authorities had to give in. Many Russian women are like that.

"But to return to my story, this child lived in the old man's house, and he sent her to a good private school. He became to her like a grandfather. They had their secrets and their jokes. Even then, he was frightfully stout, and when he took her on his knee to tell her stories, she would say, 'Please—couldn't you move back the cushion?' And with a twinkle, he would reply, 'No, my child, my sins are upon me. For sixty years I have eaten too well, and this cushion that is between us will precede me to my grave.' At first she was a sickly child, but he put her under a doctor's care until he had built up her health. She already spoke Finnish and Swedish, and later in a higher school she learned German and a little French. There she won a scholarship and so got her tuition free. Last spring she graduated high, and passed her examinations to enter a medical school for girls. But now when she was just on the point of realizing all her dreams, everything has been overturned—for the revolution makes it uncertain whether the college will open or not, and meanwhile the old man may die, and she will no longer have his aid. She is a plucky youngster, though. You see how steady she is through it all."

When she came in with the samovar, we asked her to take tea with us. She declined, but as she stood by the door she was plainly much excited still by the talk she had had with Tarasov. Again he was talking to her now, and she listened to him intensely. Her face was flushed, her speech abrupt, and so rapid that I could barely catch the drift of what she was saying.

"She wants to be a nurse," said my friend. "I am trying to argue her out of it, but the war is driving this girl insane. She is ashamed for Russia now. She feels that the war should go right on and that she must do her part. She has heard of the Women's Battalion of Death. She says she must either join with them, or be ready to nurse them when they are wounded. Look at her—what a mixing here, half boy, half girl, half woman, half child. She is barely seventeen years old."[3]

He urged her to wait for the medical school, which he still believed would open that fall. He talked to her of a doctor's career, but she interrupted sharply:

"There is no need to tell me that! To be a doctor is what I have wanted ever since I was eight years old. But what can I do? I must earn my living. Nobody should be a burden now!"

"You can easily earn your living in Petrograd, these days," he said. "You can go to the medical school and earn your expenses by work outside. You speak Swedish, and there are many rich Swedes who would take you into their offices and pay high wages for your work."

---

[3] The United States women's rights movement made progress in the years before World War I, but never considered mobilizing women for combat, until about a hundred years later than Russia. For an excellent account of the Russian fighting women, see Laurie Stoff, *They Fought for the Motherland: Russia's Women Soldiers in World War I and the Revolution* (Lawrence: University Press of Kansas, 2006.)

## CHAPTER III

"I don't want their pay!" she cried passionately. "Those Swedes are for Germany, every one! I tell you I want to help in the war! I am tired of being off on one side when such terrible things are happening! Suppose I grow up to be an old woman? How horrible it would be to look back and say, 'I was young at a time like the French Revolution, but all I did was to work for Swedes—or stay in a nice quiet place on a river!' I have come to hate this place! Here the people's tongues and ears seem shaped for petty gossip!" She stopped abruptly, breathing fast.

"My dear," said Tarasov quietly, "you will find gossip everywhere—even in the medical school. But I advise you to go there now and take a doctor's training."

"That means three years of my life," she said. He smiled:

"Even twenty is not very old."

"But I want to help, *now*," she answered, "now in the war and the revolution!" Tarasov gave a weary shrug.

"There will be plenty of time," he said. "The war and the revolution will not be settled for many years. For a whole world is fighting. Humanity is in a storm that will not settle in a day. As time goes on, all intelligent men the world over will see that the cause of freedom is centered here. Shall Germany dominate our land? If she does, the days of Rome are back—not only for us but for all Europe. I tell you the struggle will last for years—through war and peace. A new free Russia must be built, and there will be plenty of time for you—plenty of work for doctors."

Now as she listened, her brown hands were interlocked in front of her. Her face was set, and she seemed to be looking sternly ahead into the work that he described.

"I am afraid I shall never be a good doctor."

"Why not?" he asked.

"I am not strong enough."

"You look strong," he said. But the girl shook her head and exclaimed impatiently:

"Oh, it is easy to be strong in such a simple life as this! I tell you I know what lies ahead. In Russia I can see how it will be. The life of a doctor will be hard. I have dreamed of it since I was eight years old. In every dream it was always hard—and I was glad it would be like that. But now it will be harder still. And I don't want to be a doctor now unless I can be just as strong as a man—unless I can work day and night! That is the way we will have to work to build the new free Russia!" She paused a moment. "And I don't know—I am not sure." Her voice had dropped: "I had smallpox and diphtheria. It left me deaf in one ear. It left me weak in many ways."

She walked abruptly to the window, then returned to her place by the door and seemed to listen a moment. The small log house was very still.

"I haven't talked like this before to any one," she said huskily. "Please don't tell my mother."

Tarasov watched her steadily, in a tense, almost hypnotic way. "My girl, you need not worry. You are going to do fine work," he said. Her eyes met his and were held for a time, and it seemed as though some vital force were passing from him into her.

There was often something uncanny to me about this Russian friend of mine. She drew a deep breath and smiled and said:

"Yes, now I think it will be so."

"What has changed you?" he asked her, smiling back.

"You have made me remember," she replied, "that I have been lucky all my life. I worry hard—but things come right... Long ago when I worked at the theater and felt I was damning my soul for life, then came the teacher smiling and telling me it was all right And so it has been. When I dream of something very hard, some one gives it to me. Once I wanted to study singing—and I wanted it so much that I could not sleep at night But soon a fine woman came to me, who was a friend of this old man, and she gave me singing lessons free. I wanted to learn embroidery, and again she helped me out." Here the girl gave a sharp little laugh. "That was funny," she said, "for when I learned, soon it tired me to death. I was a perfect failure at that!... But in the school in Petrograd, again I was lucky," she went on. "In the schoolroom that first day I could speak no Russian. There I sat, a little Finn—and the whole room was full of girls who could speak Russian very well. I was ready to sink through a hole in the floor! But along came a woman teacher, and at once she guessed my thoughts—for I looked at her with such pain in my eyes. So she said, 'Come each morning at seven o'clock, and I will teach you until nine.' She taught me for two hours every day and in a few weeks I could speak quite well."

Again she stopped. The smile went from her face.

"That is the way it has been in my life," she ended in a resolute tone, "and that is the way it ought to be with every child in Russia. I was thinking of that tonight in the school house. Those two young girls that we took along—how happy they were! What couldn't they be if they had a chance? They must have a chance! This lazy peasant father of theirs ought to be punished by the law. They must be clothed and sent to school! Think how ashamed they were at the play. It was too hot for all of us there—and twice in the dark I loosened the heavy cloak around each child, but in a minute they wrapped them tight to hide their ragged dresses. Each one of them was bathed in sweat! And this is not right! I know what they could be! When I teach them here at night, I look at their eyes and see a light—and I tell you that is the light we need! Every child must have a chance! Every child must be lucky—get what they want—have light in their eyes!" She stopped in a breathless sort of way. "I can't say what I mean—but I know very well. We must have a new life in Russia."

She stood for a moment longer with her back against the door, her hands behind her holding the knob, short, sturdy, her strong shoulders squared, her round face set in a resolute frown.

Then abruptly she turned and left us.

# Chapter IV

## I

"I wish you had seen this neighborhood as it looked when I was a boy," Tarasov said to me one day, "the poverty, the filthy homes, the drunkenness and the disease. To you it may look poor enough still—but if you had been here in those years, you would realize what a change has come. Whenever I get discouraged, I think of two men and of what they achieved. One was the old school teacher whom we met the other night. I shall take you to see him very soon. The other is dead. He was the priest. He was not like most village priests—for as a rule they are ignorant, a dull reactionary lot. He was a most wonderful man. I shall tell you of the fight that he made.

"But first I must give you some idea of the drunkenness that existed here. When I was a child, over half the peasants would be drunk for days at a time. There were fights along the river-front. One nightmare in my memory, when I was a little boy, was of a big peasant on a raft smashing out the brains of another with a club. And this was nothing uncommon. Things had gone from bad to worse—till a bottle of vodka came to be used as a standard unit of value. When a peasant was asked what a job would cost, he would answer not in rubles but in bottles of vodka. If there was none to be had in the stores, the peasants would refuse to work, but when it came, there would be a rush to earn money to buy drink. Merchants from the larger towns came here with carts and wagons loaded down with vodka, and for this the half-crazed people parted with their grain, their cows, their very last belongings.

"As the women began to drink with the men, it caused a sex promiscuity that spread disease at a fearful rate. Many children were born idiots. In the village down by the river where we went the other night, there were almost always men and women and boys lying drunk in the ditches. One day the small steamer was just leaving dock, and a tipsy peasant boy was sitting on the rail at the stern, playing a harmonica. He lost his balance and in he went. On the wharf stood his old mother, and in her piercing voice she screeched:

"'Brothers! Hey there! Save the watch! He is wearing a watch that cost nine rubles! He will go down and stick in the mud—and the watch will be lost! Get him—get it—get the watch!' And the old woman filled the air with her yells until they fished him safely out. Then she tried to beat him, but he struck out and knocked her down.

"In the winter, every week or two, you would hear of some drunkard frozen to death. And once, when a river merchant got married and at his wedding the vodka flowed free, forty-six peasants lost their lives—for winter is no child's play here, and one must not fall asleep on the snow.

"After a Russian holiday, nearly every peasant's wife would have a black eye or a bruise. There was an old saying among them: 'He has had a fine holiday. He has been drunk from sunrise.' Toward night I could hear them coming home, men and women, singing and howling like gray wolves. Then in the dark the children would come running to my house, and knock softly and creep in and crawl under beds or into the closets. There they would stay till the yells died down and they knew that their parents were asleep.

"You often saw children drunk as well. Many of the mothers put vodka into their babies' milk. 'It is good for my baby,' one woman told me. 'See how well it makes him sleep.' Often a peasant mother would chew a mouthful of black bread, then take it out and soak it in vodka and so give it to her child.

"I remember seeing men in those days who went about wearing nothing but shirts. They had sold or pawned the rest of their clothes. And half-naked women, too, were by no means uncommon sights. Anything for alcohol. In my father's studio, which I used for a chemical laboratory, I burned wood alcohol in my lamp. One day when I was out of the room, two peasants drank up my entire can. At my rage they merely chuckled and said, 'Now, brother, we will go to sleep, and the good God will watch over us.' They ambled off together and lay down in the graveyard of the church.

"So much for the good old vodka days.

"Then a new priest came to the village. Sergei Grigorovich was his name. He had been educated in a church school in Petrograd, and he had graduated high. But then he had made a great mistake. For it was a common custom that when a young priest was given the order to go to a certain village parish and start by assisting the local priest, he should first look very carefully at the old priest's daughter, and if he did not like her, he should transfer to another parish where there was a prettier girl. For the best country church positions were commonly given as dowers with daughters of retiring priests. But this Sergei Grigorovich, a week after his graduation, very rashly married a friend of his in Petrograd, a girl without a kopeck. And so his chances were all spoiled. His superior said to him in vexation:

"'What a shame this is. You were the best student here, but now there will be nothing for you except some wretched little parish lousy with its drunkenness.'

"So, with his wife, he came to this district about thirty years ago, when I was still a boy of ten. In a village some two miles from here, he was to replace the priest who had died. This priest had been a fearful old souse. For years he had so often been too drunk to conduct any services, that the peasants had dropped the habit of ever coming to his church. Now the wretched man was dead, leaving a small and filthy hut and a little log church half tumbling down, with a field running back to the forest and all overgrown with weeds and brush, for he had been too lazy to farm. There was no parish school for the children.

"At first Sergei Grigorovich was at a loss how to begin. He had no money whatever, and only a very silly young wife, who loved him but was of little help. Nevertheless, he started in. He helped his wife to clean out the hut, and he himself repaired the church. He went into the forest with an ax and began cutting trees on the church land. Luckily he was a powerful chap. He persuaded a peasant to help him haul the logs out to the river-bank, and they started to make a brick kiln there. Other peasants stopped to watch, some grew interested in the job, and soon he had quite a few volunteers. He joked and laughed with them as they worked. A priest making bricks! It was something new. More and more peasants gathered around. They built a school house of brick and logs, and then Sergei Grigorovich collected the children from nearby. His young wife scrubbed them thoroughly and he taught them in the school. Later on, his wife and he moved over to the school to live. And she cooked lunch for the children.

"The influence of this strange young man began to spread through the neighborhood. Some of the peasants began to come, not only to church services, but between times for advice—for they had learned with great surprise that their priest had a head quite packed and crammed with all sorts of practical knowledge. He did many things for the district. The cattle and horses, as a rule, were wretched little animals. Grigorovich went to Petrograd, and there by begging all over the town he collected two hundred rubles. With this sum he secured for two months the use of a bull and a stallion, and so he began to improve the breed of livestock in our neighborhood. Again he begged money in Petrograd and bought better stocks of seeds, and with these he soon increased the crops of rye, oats and potatoes here. His wife was a Finnish girl who knew how to write Swedish, and he had her write a letter now to a model farm in Sweden, from which he got all kinds of advice on modern agriculture.

"The peasants liked him more and more, but many used to laugh at him, too, for he was so little like a priest. He was dressed like a beggar, he walked so fast and he spoke so abruptly—more like a company promoter than a solemn servant of God. 'What is his game?' they wondered. He told me that he heard one of them say, 'This priest of ours rushes along like a dog, with his gown flying out like the flag on a steamer.' He laughed at that, enjoying the joke. And he laughed at the drunkenness, sloth, and dirt.

"'Surely this generation is bad, but the next one will be better,' he said. 'First we shall improve the breed of oats and rye, of horses and cows, for that is a quicker job. Then we shall tackle the people themselves.'

"The nearest doctor in those days was miles away in the district town. There was disease in plenty here, plagues and epidemics, and there were frequent accidents on barges and in quarries. Grigorovich thought it would be a fine thing if in every hamlet there was at least one woman or girl who could give first aid treatment. So he went to the doctor in the town. He went in his ragged old black gown, and kneeled and kissed the doctor's feet. 'Help us, brother, for Christ's sake.' He persuaded the doctor to come twice a week to his school and teach the older girls. And in less than a year, in every one of the seven little villages belonging to his parish, there was a girl who knew at least something of how to take care of the injured or sick.

"Then Sergei Grigorovich went to a prosperous peasant, who had made quite a lot of money by manufacturing quick-lime, and after much entreating he persuaded the man for the glory of God to build a dispensary. It was built of brick, not far from the church. And there some forty peasant girls worked as volunteer nurses, under a head matron and the doctor from the town. In the meantime the priest had found that women in childbirth often died because they had no one to help them but neighbors as ignorant as themselves. So he persuaded the doctor's wife, who was herself a midwife, to come over and teach his girl nurses. By this time they began to be known as 'The Village Sisters of Mercy.' When a woman gave birth to a child, the doctor or his wife would be there, and after that, for a week or two, one of the young Sisters would go every day to the woman's hut, do the house work for her, tend to the baby and see that all was done as the doctor had directed.

"About this time, Grigorovich began to get after the drunkards. He came to me one night with a plan. It was now ten years since his beginning, and I was a student in Petrograd. I was taking a chemical course, and when I came home in the summer I used to make experiments, in which the priest would join like a boy. I shall never forget his eager black eyes. Well, on this night he proposed to me an experiment on the drunkards. He said that the doctor approved of it, and I was quite ready to join in.

"'We must do this job in a scientific way,' said Grigorovich solemnly, but with a twinkle in his eye. 'We must,' I replied. And in Petrograd I bought for him a stomach pump. With this we went after the drunkards in a way that terrified their souls. Most of our crimes were committed at night, and our victims bellowed like young bulls. 'Their stomachs shall be whiter than snow,' the priest declared, and he worked with a will. Then he gave them medicine which his friend, the doctor, had prescribed. And after that, the mere smell of vodka was a terror to their souls.

"The priest drove on with his crusade. In the church, he preached against vodka without quoting a word from the gospel. He gave only medical facts. And this was a terrible scandal. 'Heathen lectures in our church!' If the doctor happened to be there, the priest would stop in the midst of his sermon to ask the doctor a question or two and so amplify his words. The peasants opened their mouths like dogs at this chap and his new religion!

"But most of the intelligent ones had come to support him now. Everything he had done for them had been on a basis of give and take. 'You help the church and I'll help you.' With their aid he rebuilt his church; then he erected a larger school; and later he started building, in each of the seven villages, schools and churches under one roof. Most of these were made of stone. He used boulders for the walls and hewn timber for the furniture. He loved to work with ax or saw, and to plow and harrow on his field.

"But beneath all this, remember, was a man of deep refinement. Often he would come to our house, and in my father's studio he would talk about paintings half the night. I remember once at daybreak I was aroused by my mother's voice scolding them for not going to bed. He was a jovial fellow. He loved to go to the country balls and dance with the very prettiest girls, with his black frock waving behind him, his long hair over his shoulders swinging violently about. He loved good horses; it was his joy to borrow a horse and drive very fast. The peasants liked him more and more; they called him now 'our gypsy priest.'

"He knew how to get on with all sorts and conditions—even with the corrupt officials of the former government. Once when he wanted money, he went to the police inspector in the district town and said in a confidential tone,

"'Look here, brother, in your work I know you have taken money which had much better go to God. If you square up accounts with Him and give five hundred rubles for a new church, think how much easier you will feel.' The inspector gave him the money but looked gloomy at the loss—for he was a fat man who loved his wine. Then the priest said sadly, 'I was wrong. The gift has not made you feel easy enough. I think you had better give me now so much money that you can smile.' The inspector broke into a laugh at this, and slapped the priest on the back, and said, 'You are a real man, brother!' And he gave five hundred more!

"On the other hand, Grigorovich was very careful not to attract the attention of the government to his many village reforms—for all progressive men in those days were apt to get on the list of 'suspects' and so be allowed to do nothing at all. He shunned the word 'progressive.' Once a Petrograd journalist came out to write about his work, but Sergei Grigorovich in alarm begged him not to write a word. 'I am not a progressive,' he said, 'but just a plain simple man in the village doing some things for the love of Christ.'

"He still looked like a beggar man. When he needed money he would go to Petrograd, and kneel and kiss the very feet of the people who could help him. He also earned quite a bit himself by conducting funerals in one of the city graveyards there. He used to joke about it. 'I grab money from the dead,' he said, 'to use it for the living.'

"He never stopped working day or night. He was to be seen at all hours striding about the countryside. If a peasant was dying, the priest was there; if a child was born, the priest was there. So he used up his life in twenty-five years. He came here at twenty-two and died at forty-seven. Meanwhile, a generation had passed, and he had fulfilled his promise. For a new generation had grown up and the life of the district had been changed."

## 2

Tarasov took me one afternoon to the village where the priest had lived. It was an uneven row of huts halfway down the river-bank, in which were jagged limestone quarries. There was a kiln for quick-lime here, and a score of women and boys were loading the lime onto a barge, in clumsy little barrows which they trundled up a plank. A few old fishing dories had been pulled up on the muddy bank, and some fishing nets had been spread out to dry. From the top of the slope a small green meadow extended back to the forest.

Up there was the hospital Sergei Grigorovich had built, a long low structure made of brick. We found it nearly deserted. One of the village Sisters of Mercy, a peasant girl in Red Cross garb, showed us the dispensary and the two wards of five beds each. There were only two or three patients left. The war had stopped their work, she said. No more money and no supplies—so they would have to close it down. Not far away was the small church, of plaster painted white and green. The brick school house stood close by, and it was but a few steps from there to the stout square building of brick and logs which had been both home and school in the early years when the priest made his start. It stood like a little fortress, built to last for eternity. The walls were nearly four feet thick. There was a basement of three low rooms where the priest and his wife had lived, and two large sunny rooms above which he had reserved for the children. In the rear was the little old hut of his drunken predecessor. It was used as a stable now. There was a barn, a vegetable garden and a dark green field of rye.

We dropped in for a talk with the new priest, who was living here with his handsome young wife, his sister and two children. They occupied both floors of the house. I was attracted from the start by the high spirits of this little family. There were giggles and laughter as we came in, and Tarasov was greeted joyously. As for me, I was a sensation. A writer from America, come to interview the priest! We were ushered into the living room, fresh and clean with its plastered walls, which were painted a light blue. There were high-backed chairs with "tidies," a sofa, and a table covered with a red velvet cloth. The priest was an affable little man, dressed in a brown linen robe. His head was nearly bald in front, but his hair fell over his shoulders behind. His age was about thirty-five. He had a funny tuft of a beard and he wore gold glasses on his nose, with twinkling eyes behind them. His features radiated health, high spirits, animation. His talk was pointed by quick gestures and by large expansive smiles.

"The revolution," he declared, "has been a splendid thing for the church. But it was not all so smooth at first, for the people looked upon the priests as the hated officials of the Czar. On the fifth of March the peasants came rushing into my churchyard. Many of them were young rowdies who had not come to worship for years. They were in a furious mood.

"'Holy ground,' they shouted, 'is no place to speak with a devil like you!' And they told me to come to the school house and give them an accounting of what I had

## CHAPTER IV

done with the church funds. I saw an ugly time ahead. I said goodbye to my wife and children, for I was sure I would be killed. In the school the peasants all began to shout at me: 'Show us your books and your accounts! If any money stuck to your fingers, we will swing you to a tree!'

"To reply to them, let me tell you, was a very difficult job. I have always detested bookkeeping. My books had been kept for me by a clerk, who used to come from the district town—and now as I held them in my hands, I could make nothing of them. All the time that peasant mob kept up the threats and insults:

"'See how he trembles, the guilty dog! Let us smash in his skull for him, and find what guilty thoughts are there!'

"I tried to explain as best I could, but they would have none of it. Soon they all crowded around one chap who knew how to write, and he wrote a petition to Petrograd demanding that I be thrown out of the church as an enemy of God and the people. That was a very trying day, and when at night they let me go, I was utterly exhausted.

"The peasants now felt themselves wholly free, and my position in those days was like that of a man standing near a great dog who has just broken his chain in a rage, and is barking, and has not decided yet whether he shall leap on the man and tear him all to pieces, or whether he shall simply jump for joy because he is free. After the strain upon my nerves, I dropped into a stupor of complete indifference. Everything was so uncertain. How could I go on with my work? The peasants still kept watching my house as though they thought I might try to escape. They would follow me when I walked out and shout all manner of abuse. Meanwhile they kept sending more petitions to Petrograd. There was no response, because in that city the new leaders were too absorbed in politics to stop for the church. But out here in my little parish, the whole revolution in those days centered around this house of God, for it had been the very heart of life for themselves and their children.

"Well, as I waited, little by little the trouble in my soul disappeared. Slowly I began to see the great good in the revolution. I felt as though old handcuffs, that had rusted into the bones of my wrists, had now suddenly fallen off, that I was free from the Old Regime and that I could work for God as I chose. I prayed to Him to show me the way, and in a dream I received this message: 'Carefully read the creed of your church.' I did so, until I came to the words, 'I believe in one congregational church.' And then I saw what I must do. For that word 'congregational' was God's answer to my prayer. I must bring, the peasants back into the church reorganized in such a way that they should feel they could run it themselves and make it a part of the revolution.

"Now I walked all over my parish. I entered every hut and said, 'You must run the house of God yourselves. You must come and hold a meeting there.' And they told me they would come. Then I went home and anxiously planned. Each one of the seven hamlets should elect two delegates, I resolved, and these fourteen should form my board. But how manage the elections in the best and speediest way? I resolved on having a secret ballot. And this mere technical detail, when the day of the meeting arrived, proved to be my salvation. For the peasants were as interested and pleased as children with a new toy.

"'This is a mighty smart trick!' they declared. 'Why have we not thought of it before? When we used to elect our starosta or decide any question in the mir, what a lot of shouting we did! The fellow who could bawl the loudest was the one who carried the day. If a bull could have been at our meetings, his view would certainly have prevailed!' Then an old wolf of a peasant growled out, 'At a meeting in my village, the whole discussion was broken up by a fool with a big harmonica. Right into the crowd he marched. As he played, he sang at the top of his lungs. The girls and boys sang with him, and so the whole meeting came to an end.' Another one, a woman, said, 'But now just see how smooth it works. You choose your man inside of your soul, and God alone knows who it is. Into the box you drop his name, and your husband cannot beat you for not having given him your vote!'

"Well, so the peasants were greatly pleased with my secret ballot plan. Less than half of them knew how to write, but I helped the others out, and so they elected their delegates. They chose four women and ten men. I soon called a meeting of the new board, and sitting around a table here they dived into the mysteries of accounting and bookkeeping, and when they could understand nothing at all, they began to show me sympathy.

"'You have a hard job here,' they said.

"'I did have it,' I replied. 'But now it is yours.' They looked very uneasy.

"'We do not want it,' one of them said. 'It was you who came and called us together to take a share in the life of the church.'

"'But this is your share,' I told them, 'to control the property, and leave the affairs of the soul to your priest.'

"And I have stuck to this point ever since. I refuse to haggle with the man who cuts the firewood for the church; I refuse to decide the wages of the old woman who cleans out the school. In this year of revolution and strikes, I have had a little strike of my own, and with the result I am quite content.

"Well, in addition to such jobs my board of laymen has done other things. Not long ago they chose one of their number to be sent to Petrograd, to a national church assembly there. In this choice, too, they were greatly pleased to use the secret ballot. First I carefully explained how a great all-Russian assembly was to be held to consider the plan for a new and democratic church. Then I let them elect their man, and very solemnly they chose a wise old peasant fisherman.

"Again, about two weeks ago we faced a critical problem. For in Petrograd the new Ministry of Education had announced that it would soon take away from the church its thirty-five thousand parish schools and manage them like all the rest. No compulsory teaching of God's word! When I came across this sinful plan, I called together not only my board but my whole congregation here, and had them vote on the question. By a vote of two hundred to seventeen they decided: 'If God's law is not taught, we will not send our children to school.' At the meeting a peasant soldier, who had lost an arm in battle, suddenly arose and said,

"'God's law must be taught to my children, or else they will grow up wild as hawks! And it must be done at the nation's expense. Everything else that is taught in the school is paid for by the nation, and God's law is most important of all—for without it a man is only a beast!'

"When he sat down you could see them all nodding their heads in approval. I remember one old woman in front who kept nodding long after the others were through, and whispering quickly with tears in her eyes: Then I rose and talked to my people.

"'You must think this out very clearly,' I said. 'If the Government supports our church, what of the other religious sects? Shall they be supported, too? Remember this is a new free land where all men should be treated well. Shall the Lutheran pastors and the Polish Catholic priests, Jewish rabbis, Mohammedan Mullahs, be supported by the State?' The wounded soldier rose and declared,

"'In the new free Russia, brothers, all must be allowed to worship God and the Saints in their own way. And therefore all these men should be paid.'

"He sat down, and most of them said, 'He is right.' But without standing up an old peasant called out:

"'The money that the Government spends is nothing but our taxes. We must not waste it foolishly. And so in each village the people must meet and choose what church they want the most. Then let us support that church, but no others. It would cost too much for us to have four or five religions here!'

"So the speeches went on, showing shrewd good sense and a deep conviction of the need of religious education. And I was very happy that night. For truly religious instruction is the very foundation of life. They claim it is a needless expense to teach God's law in the government schools—but remember that in a human existence there come two terrible moments which are as vital as all the other thousands of days and nights in a life. These two moments are birth and death, and there is a dark mystery in them both, which only religion can fill with light. People say that a certain man has been taken up to Paradise. Where is that? I believe it is not in the skies, for I remember the words of Christ, 'The Kingdom of God is within you.' It is like a great warm light which He keeps burning in our souls. And only He can keep it bright.

"I hear that in France and England they try to give moral teaching to children without any real belief in God. But you cannot go very far with a child if you appeal to his reason alone. Go and hear a machine piano play, and then a real musician. Both play the same piece of music, but what a difference there is! And there is the same gap between the morals of children brought up by mere logic and those reared in the love of Christ. On such love all our social duties should be founded as on rock. If every man and woman and child has a kingdom of God within him, then we shall never again have a Czar, for this will raise our people to such a state of enlightenment that Russia will be a free brotherhood and never again an autocracy.

"Yes, I am for the revolution, glad the Old Regime is gone. When I was in Petrograd last year, the Czar's police would jeer at me. 'Look at this long-haired man of God,' I heard one of them say on the street. 'For years these priests have preached against vodka. Men went on boozing just the same. But then our Little Father, the Czar, stopped it all with one stroke of his pen. The real power is in the law.'

"But those ignorant brutes have been thrown out, for we want no more of these Czar commands. Now all must be done by man's free will, and it must be the work of the church to make this will a power for good and for the happiness of all. So the priest in this parish before me worked. He used no force or repression, he simply worked by argument and good deeds for the love of Christ. And what happiness he brought to men!

"Another good thing in the revolution is that it has set free all religions. The Orthodox Church and the Old Believers, Catholics, Lutherans, Buddhists, Mohammedans, Jews, all have their chance. And that will be a good thing for us, for they have much that we can learn. For example, we say that a man is born sinful and must be washed clean—but the Buddhist says just the opposite. He declares that the whole world is a bright and glorious miracle, and man is the diamond of it all. I like such doctrine; it is fine! It used to be in our own church, too; for Christ, the Great Brother, preached joy and not gloom. The gloom was a trick of our government, for the purpose of keeping the people down.

"All real socialists should be our friends. Their aim, the welfare of the body, should go hand in hand with ours, which is the welfare of the soul. You cannot blame the peasants here for keeping their minds on material things, for they live in wretched poverty still, and only when this poverty is lifted off their shoulders can they straighten up like men. In this we must help. We are already planning a new education for our young priests. They will be taught not only religion, but also the practical sciences, agriculture, economics, medicine, sanitation—anything that can be of use to the daily life of the village. We need athletic sports and games to attract the young people to the church. I have read of how they do such things in your American churches which seem to be driving rapidly along the same road which we must take.

"Already our Russian priests are beginning to drop the unnatural tone of voice that was used in conducting the service. Now every word must be understood. We want no more needless mystery. We shall have a hard enough time as it is, to make simple and clear in the peasant's mind the connection between the new free Russia and the reorganized Church of Christ. We must show how the old saints were really the first socialists, the pioneers who not only worked for the souls of the people but helped them to cooperate and do better farming, too. The stories of such holy men must be told in church to the peasants, and linked with the names of Edison, Cartwright, and Pasteur, and other modern pioneers.

"And of course our church must clean its house. The corrupt and impure monks must be thrown out of the monasteries, and they must be made places where the monks work for the people as the saints did in the past. As yet, the monks, who are called the Black Priests, have shown little sign of sympathy for the new free Russia. It is the White Priests in the parishes who are leading the movement of progress now, and there may be a great struggle soon between the Black Priests and the White. For we White Priests are the ones who are close to the village life, and only by keeping close to the people will the Russian Church live on.[1]

"And this is as it should be. For in the beginning the Great Brother said, 'I am not the God of the dead, but of the living.'"

## 3

Soon after that, we started home, and as we strolled up the river-bank, Tarasov asked what I thought of the priest. "A bit too rosy," I replied, "in his view of the church and what it can do. I keep thinking of the priests I've seen in other Russian villages, in Petrograd and Moscow. About nine out of ten appeared to me an ignorant stupid lot of men, who would ask for nothing better than a return to the Old Regime."

"Nevertheless," said Tarasov, "this fellow is significant. He is one of the younger priests, who have been reached by the influences of the last twelve years. For Russia has never been the same since the first revolution in 1905." He turned and studied my face for a moment. "What is the matter?" he inquired.

"It's hard to put it in words," I replied, "but your jolly little priest back there—well, he did not seem to me to have got very deep into life. I should like to have met the other one—the ragged chap who chopped down trees, made bricks and used the stomach pump, worked and begged and danced—and died. His successor seemed to me to be talking out of books. He's all right so far as he goes—but somehow, here in Russia, I'm always expecting something—something a good deal deeper than that." Tarasov lit a cigarette and I noticed a curious glint in his eyes.

"I shall show you something deeper," he said. And when I asked him what he meant, he replied, "The village sorcerer."

On the following Sunday, we went back to the little church, which stood on the edge of the forest. The bells were already jangling, and the narrow dirt road on the river-bank was dotted by hurrying figures. At the gate of the churchyard, two

---

[1] In contrast to the Roman Catholic Church, the Orthodox Church divided its clergy into two parts: the Black clergy, or monks who took vows of celibacy, and the White clergy, who administered to the populace in churches. The latter could marry and often became part of the village, farming church lands, etc.

old beggars stood bowing low and muttering their appeals for alms. In a long open shed nearby stood a row of carts and horses. The service was about to begin. Some of the men had gone inside; others were sitting on the grass smoking pipes or cigarettes. They were dressed in sober black or gray, with trousers tucked into their high boots. A few wore colored blouses. Here and there under the somber fir trees stood huge wooden crosses, some white and some a faded blue. Each one marked a peasant's grave. Presently a young woman in black, with a small girl clinging to her hand, came hurrying in through a side gate. They went straight to a new-made grave with a soldier's cap upon its cross, and standing there with heads bowed low they prayed devoutly for the dead, crossing themselves from time to time. The widow looked barely twenty years old. Her broad face was impassive. They turned and went quietly into the church.

Over near the hitching shed, stood a high swing for the children, and three jolly little boys were swinging there—two in white blouses, the other in red. Their feet were bare. Watching them, on the grass nearby sat two young Austrian prisoners who were smoking cigarettes. We went over and joined them. They were Hungarian mountaineers who had been taken prisoner on the great Brusilov drive down into the Carpathians. At first they had worked in Siberia, lumbering in the forests. Now they were loading barges here. They were paid the same wages as Russians, they said, and were free to go about. They seemed to be quite satisfied. These were good people, they declared. There were some fine girls in the village. On the whole they were having a very good time, and doubted if they would ever go home.

"I don't care to live in my country," said one, "till the Germans get out. They are trying to manage everything there." The other one asked if America had declared war on Austria yet. "No," I replied, "but it's bound to happen soon if your country stays in the war." He scowled and said he was sorry. He had a married brother living in Pennsylvania.

A moment later we left them, for the peasants all around us were throwing looks of suspicion our way.

The church was of white plaster, with a green roof and a dome of gold. We found it crowded with people inside. The walls were white, the vaulted ceiling was blue with gold stars, and there was much gold and tinsel about. Painted saints looked down from the walls, and there were many candles burning. Wreaths of incense hung in the air. In front, beside the little priest, stood the huge old peasant deacon, who was slowly intoning the service in a deep and thrilling bass. Both the deacon and the priest were dressed in stiff brocaded robes. The responses were being sung by a peasant choir of boys and girls. We went outside and sat listening. Through the open windows, the music poured in waves of sound, with a crude sweet yearning beauty, as though pleading for Holy Russia with God.

A soldier sat near us on the grass. He looked hardly more than a boy. His rough boots were broken, gray with mud; his uniform was dirty and torn; his face was unshaven, and in his eyes was a look half sullen, half bewildered. He took a cigarette from my friend, but he was in no mood to talk. No, he had not deserted, he said, he was here on leave from Petrograd. But it was hard to tell what to do. Every one said something different.

"Some fellows say to go on with the war; others say to stop fighting now. Some are shouting, 'Kill the rich.' Others say that will do us no good. And nobody knows and nothing is sure. All is mixed up and nothing is clear.... . And here they are singing, and how do I know? Is there a God or is this all a lie?"

The youngster heaved a heavy sigh, threw away his cigarette, lay back in the grass and folded his arms tight over his eyes. Those eyes and the low fierce note in his voice had given me such an impression of groping and anxiety, that as I looked down on him he had my genuine sympathy. But all at once, very softly, this Russian youth began to snore.

A gray bearded peasant came out of the church, with a heavy pewter plate in his hands, and began to pass the collection among the people in the yard. When he came to the sleeping soldier, he stirred the boy angrily with his foot. "This is no place for your snoozing!" he muttered. "You ought to be fighting and winning the war!"

The lad jumped up, with an angry scowl, went shambling out of the churchyard and disappeared into the forest nearby.

For a few moments longer we sat listening to the singing. Then Tarasov touched my arm. "Look," he said to me softly. "You asked for something very deep. It is standing over by the gate."

## 4

I saw a short, gnarled figure there, an old man leaning on a stick. Upon his thick gray shock of hair a soft brown hat was pushed far back. His face was tanned and wrinkled, his eyes so sharp that I noticed them even from across the yard. "His name," said Tarasov, "is Kraychok—which in English means Wild Duck. It's lucky for you that he's still alive. There were thousands like him in the villages once, but now they are rapidly dying out and he is one of the last of his kind. He is the village sorcerer."

As we drew near, he did not see us—for his head was turned to one side, and as the music from the choir drifted out from the church nearby, in his black eyes was a glint of amusement He was watching a horse in the hitching shed who was trying very carefully to reach a fly with his hind leg. When the old man caught sight of Tarasov, a smile leaped over his grim face. A vigorous handshake, a few gruff words, and then abruptly he led the way out of the little churchyard and off along the river-bank.

"We are going to his hut," said my friend. "And I shall tell you about him first. He will not mind if I leave him out of the conversation now, for he likes to be left to himself.

"I met him through my father. My father, as a peasant boy, went to school in the monastery just across the river, and what he did not learn from the monks he learned through Kraychok, his close friend. Kraychok was then a wild little lad who lived in the same hut in the forest to which he is taking us today. In those early years his father was there, and he was also a sorcerer. He taught the two boys many things, dark mysteries of forest life. He was a great hunter and trapper, and a man of such strange power, too, that he could weave hypnotic spells. Time passed and this old hunter died. Meanwhile the two lads grew up. My father became a painter and he used to paint the peasants here—his old friend Kraychok most of all. In his studio they had long talks, and I used to listen, a scared little boy. I remember nothing that I heard, for it was such a fearful thing to be listening to a sorcerer, that his gruff words would often be a mere jumble in my ears.

"Kraychok was a hunter. You see the cartridge belt at his side. In those days he would disappear into the forest for weeks at a time, and there, the peasants used to say, he communed with the powers of darkness, as his father and his grandfather had done many years before. But all that he learned of such forces he used only for the people's good. He employed his miraculous power against the so-called Evil Eye. When it cast its baneful spell on some frightened woman or child, every one knew that Kraychok could break that spell if he so pleased. And even though he was greatly feared, he was deeply liked by the peasants, for he was almost always ready to use his power in their behalf.

"My father painted him many times. One picture hung in the studio when I was still a little chap, and often when the room was empty toward the evening, I would steal in through the open door and look at it fearfully in the dusk. Suddenly with a cold rush of fear I would scamper into a corner and hide, with my face pressed close against the log wall. But soon I would come slowly back and gaze up wondering as before.

"I learned about the sorcerer, too, from my aged grandmother. Although not superstitious (for she was a great reader of Voltaire), she was constantly being surprised and disturbed by the things this simple hunter could do. At a sick bed in some peasant's hut, she had seen him stop a flow of blood by the slow hypnotic words he spoke and the strange power in his eyes. In this way he worked many miraculous cures—of a kind that since have been explained by Charcot in Paris.[2]

"As I grew older, Kraychok took me into the forest to hunt. One day, I remember, after he had been telling some stories of enchantment, he stopped short and said to

---

[2] Jean-Martin Charcot (1825–93) was a French neurologist known especially for his teaching on hypnosis and hysteria. It is interesting that people in rural Russia were aware of his work.

## CHAPTER IV

me, 'Now, Juvenale Ivanovich, put your shotgun on the ground and I will show you something.' I put down my gun, and in a voice with a gathering power in it, he said, 'Walk across this clearing, and be sure you don't look back!' So I walked along. The ground was smooth, quite level. Yet suddenly I felt as though my feet had struck on something. I stumbled and pitched forward. In a great fright I rose and looked back, and there, ten steps behind me, stood the old man laughing—in such a way that he made no sound. There was sweat upon his forehead and an exhausted look in his eyes.

"'Ah, Juvenale Ivanovich,' he said to me softly, 'see how you fell down suddenly on such a nice smooth piece of ground.'

"I stared at him, then ran away, but in a few minutes I came back and begged him to tell me how he had done it.

"'First,' he explained, in that same low voice, 'I got you into just the right mood, for that is very important. Then I told you to walk along, and I came softly close behind. I put my own soul into yours. And suddenly I made myself feel as though I had stumbled and fallen down. If I do this with absolute certainty, then nothing can stop you from doing so, too.

"He used this power constantly. He would employ it in love affairs. He could make boys and girls fall in love with each other, or out again, whenever he chose. But never would he do this for money; he intervened in such affairs only when sure he was doing good. He made many matches in this way and broke up many betrothals. He employed his power, too, on the sick—not only through hypnotic force but also through herbs in the forest, which his father had taught him to use."

After that, Tarasov talked with Kraychok for a time. Then presently we came to his home, on the edge of a wood of birches and firs. A small hut of old brown logs, it was lined with skins inside; there were dried plants on the floor; herbs hung from the low rafters, and by a rude couch in a corner was a small black iron pot in which he brewed his medicines.

"He has little use for his medicines now," Tarasov told me, "for the doctor from the town has slowly but steadily taken his place. The doctor, the school teacher, and the priest have gradually shoved him to the wall. That is why he is so silent. He keeps thinking of the past."

The old man had sat down on the couch and was watching us with grim, curious eyes.

"While he brewed," continued Tarasov, "he kept repeating to himself strange words that he had been taught by his father. As a student I wrote some of them down, and from a professor in Petrograd I learned that they were mutilated fragments of a language nearly extinct belonging to the distant East. He chanted these words in a low sad voice."

At a word from my friend, the hunter rose and took down from the wall a long flintlock gun. It was carefully wrapped in old red cloths. These he removed, and without speaking handed the weapon over to me. The barrel was inlaid with silver, and faintly engraved upon it were words in some Far Eastern tongue. Kraychok returned to his seat on the couch.

"He used to tell me," Tarasov said, "that this gun was once enchanted. It had such a quality that if you wished to kill any beast you had only to think of such a beast and it would appear before you. Moreover, when you fired, the bullet was certain to find its mark. His father and his grandfather had hunted with it all their lives. Hence their fame as hunters here. But for himself the spell of it was broken by the act of a friend. This friend, a neighboring peasant lad, was in love with a certain village girl, but a handsome stranger came along, and the girl soon ran away with him. The discarded peasant lover came in a fury to Kraychok's hut. Kraychok was away at the time. The friend took the gun and went into the forest, and there he repeated to himself, I wish to see this man and girl! I wish to see this man and girl!'—till suddenly they both appeared. He pulled the trigger. The man fell dead and the girl vanished instantly into the air. But then was heard a beastly laugh, and out of the shadows were bellowed these words: 'From today this gun shall have no charm!' And so it has happened, Kraychok says. A mere relic now, it hangs on the wall."

Presently we left the hut, and with the hunter leading the way, we took a path that led still deeper into the cool dim forest. Tarasov talked to him for a while, but he walked on without reply. "I am trying to persuade him," my friend explained, turning to me, "to take us to his favorite haunt. Perhaps he will. I am not sure. The best way is to leave him to walk ahead, and let him take us or not, as he wills."

"Tell me some more about him," I said. And Tarasov told this story:

"He used to say there are many places where great treasure is hidden here. To get it, you must go and find a certain magic flower. In the forest is a plant upon which such a flower blooms, once a year on the Eve of St. John's [Day]. You must find this plant and mark the spot—and on that mysterious evening, exactly at midnight, you must be there. Around you you must mark three circles with a stick, to keep off evil spirits. Then you must sit down quietly and listen for the smallest sound. You must work up your courage to a pitch where you will not fear anything—for, as the fiery flower blooms, great creatures creep up from the bowels of the earth and with hideous cries stretch out their claws to seize the seething flower of flame. You must snatch it first—and keep up your courage. For if you are a good Christian, he says, no one of these devils can do you harm. You must hold the flower like a torch, look down into the heaving earth, and when you see where the treasure lies, you must dig quickly with your spade—for if you remain in that spot too long, the fiery flower will burn out and leave you in the hellish night.

"He had learned all this from his father, who told him that some day he would meet an evil spirit in the wood, and that this ghost would lead him for days in great circles into the forest. Then at last he would hear a laugh, and by that he would know he had reached the spot where the treasure lay buried in the earth.

## CHAPTER IV

"Well, and so it happened. Kraychok one day saw a shape of mist, and he felt a breath impelling him on. So he strayed in circles for many days. Nor was he tired or distressed, for the ghost was excellent company, whispering in a voice like a breeze the most amusing jokes and tales. At last a sudden laugh rang out, and instantly Kraychok stood quite still, for he knew he had reached the magic spot. It was a wild place, a swamp full of huge weeds at the foot of a hill, with the river flowing by below. As he was standing motionless there, looking intently all about, a strange feeling of certainty came upon him in a wave—and he knew which one of those weeds was the plant on which the fiery flower would bloom.

"He returned to his home and there resolved to make the awful venture.

"So, upon the Eve of St. John's, Kraychok started from his hut. As he had been told by his father to do, he took in his pocket a hunk of black bread that had been made without any salt, and he put his right boot on his left foot and vice versa. From his hut he walked out slowly backwards, and by good luck, he told me, he bumped into no passer-by—for if he had, the spell would have been broken. Off he walked alone through the wood, and after many hours he came to the mystic swamp.

"He drew three circles, said some prayers and tried to make his heart feel strong. Just exactly at midnight, on the plant which he was watching, came a little gleam of fire. It blossomed like a tiny spark, and then before old Kraychok's eyes it grew into a flower of flame. As he jumped to seize it in his hand, he heard in the thick darkness terrific yells and bellows, pounding hoofs. From the hill an enormous boulder came rolling down upon him. He sprang to one side, and with a roar it crashed through the trees and down the bank and fell into the river. Big waves dashed against the banks. And the heart of Kraychok grew like ice, for now he heard a teasing laugh and a thick bestial voice that said,

"'You will never go forth alive, my friend.'

"He did not know how he should get away. Again he drew three circles, and he prayed to the good God to make strong his heart and protect him on this night of miracles. The howls and bellows still went on; tall pine trees came crashing down. In the blackness and the noise he lost his grip on the flower of flame. It flickered and died; all light was gone. He fell unconscious on the ground.

"When he woke up, the day had come. He felt very weak and as though in a fever. He crept down to the river and drank like a dog, and ate his black unsalted bread. He wandered in circles, losing his way, but at last in the evening he came back home."

Soon after Tarasov had finished this yarn, the old man walking in front of us turned and said something to my friend. We sat down by a tree and smoked for a while, and by dint of a little urging we drew from him another tale which he recounted slowly, in a gruff low monotonous voice, stopping at times and waiting while Tarasov translated for me.

"On Ladoga Lake there is a green island which lies very low," he said. "Just a green speck on the water it is. But once there were terrible wonders there. Then the peasants and the fishermen came out in boats from the village on shore. They brought a priest to the island and had a religious procession, and prayed to Christ to stop such things, such witcheries of ancient times. So the miracles were stopped, but you found the echoes still. For a priest can stop some witcheries, but where human blood has been darkly shed, where the soul has been torn from the body without confession or chance to repent, the spirit of the victim must always walk about the place where the body is slowly rotting away. It is hard for such a soul, for the evil ghosts all follow him. You hear the laughter of devils, the groans of the tormented one; you hear its slow heavy steps go by.

"So it was on that small island. When I went to hunt wild ducks and geese, sometimes when I had finished my hunting I would lie like a dead man on the beach all stiff and cold—while secrets were revealed to me—and the autumn clouds swept over the sky."

Old Kraychok paused for a long time, staring off among the trees. At last he continued softly:

"But then some smart young students from the college in the town came out to hunt ducks on that green island, and they brought me as their guide. They had heard of the ancient wonders, but they laughed and declared they felt at their ease. Town people never believe such things. Few of them have any faith in devils—or even in God and the Holy Saints. This is because they are taught so much in their foolish little colleges, and they read so much in newspapers and books, that their souls grow hard and dry, and become like crowded little rooms. How can such mighty figures as God, the Saints, the Devils, enter into such small rooms? So these people can believe nothing at all.

"When these fellows came to the island, I told them of no miracles, and neither did the fishermen, for what was the use of trying to tell such things to empty-headed folk? They decided to stay several days. They made fun of the rumor that spirits were here. At night they would show how brave they could be. So the fishermen left us some sails and ropes, and with these we made a tent upon a level sandy beach. We had a good day's hunting; we came back tired to the camp and had some supper, and after that we all lay down in the tent to sleep. The young men tried to tease me about my belief in ghosts—but I said nothing in reply, for as I lay next to the side of the tent, already I felt some figure pressing against me from outside. I felt a cold breath pass over my face, and I told myself,

"'Now it begins. Let us see how these learned fellows will feel.'

"They had stopped talking suddenly. One by one they rose up and went out of the tent, and there in whispers they confessed how some figure had pressed on the ribs of each one. As we listened, we heard heavy steps on the sand and groans like those of the winter's wind, and we heard strange laughter, too. Then these men from the college grew quite cold and white with fear. I alone knew how to destroy the spell. I told them all to listen, while I began to repeat a prayer which I had learned from a very old monk. And at once the evil voices ceased." The old man paused. He sat motionless, with his back against a tree. "And then they went back to their college," he said.

He seemed to have forgotten us now. He was looking at the ground. He plucked up a small plant with pink berries and began to study it closely. Meanwhile, Tarasov told me,

"I knew one of the fellows who made up that camping party. He was a medical student then, and later he became the head of a college of veterinary surgeons. He said that everything happened that night exactly as Kraychok describes. His explanation of it was that the old man's belief in the spirits was so strong, intense and real, that by hypnotic power he imparted it to the rest.

"This hypnotic power of his was amazingly strong," Tarasov said. "As I have already told you, he employed it on the sick. And for something over thirty years he attended women in childbirth. He would come to a woman confined, and would stand by her bed and look into her eyes, and slowly stroking her head, he would say, 'All is still well. You don't feel any pain.' He would repeat these words many times, in a voice so kind and soothing, no one could have imagined that such a dirty uncouth man could speak in such a tender way. I have watched the women's faces, and if they did feel any pain, they gave no evidence of it at all. I asked him once where he got this power. He said that in his family it had been handed down from father to son for generations.[3]

"'It came from the depths of the forest,' he said. Into a certain forest glade he would go and lie like a dead man, and into his spirit would pour the strength of the living soul of this Russian land, a soul made up of the spirits of many strange dark peoples who used to live here long ago. Only in that one spot in the forest is he able to feel the past. I am going to ask him to take us there."

When Tarasov spoke to him, at first the old hunter did not reply. Then suddenly he rose and said, "We shall go." And he started up the path. We walked for some moments in silence. It was not far, Tarasov said. My curiosity deepening, I asked what kind of a place it was.

"Quite empty and silent," he replied. "But you told me you wanted something deeper than the religion of the priest. I think you will see and feel it here." We came into a clearing of two or three acres, surrounded by tall silent pines. In the center was what I took to be a high narrow mound about eighty feet long, all tufted with green grass and weeds. But in order to get a better look, we climbed a hummock not far away—and there for some time we stood perfectly still. For from this point the mound appeared as a prodigious granite figure, hewn with a crude terrific art to depict a woman in childbirth.

After the silence, Tarasov said,

---

[3] This story reminds one of the reputation of another "holy man," Grigory Rasputin, who was believed to have the ability to cure Alexis, the son of Nicholas II, of hemophilia, apparently by the use of hypnosis.

"Very few of the peasants will ever come here. Kraychok says that he heard of it first from his father—who told him only a part. So much secret knowledge, he sadly declares, has been lost forever to the world by this process of handing it down by word of mouth from father to son. This figure has been here, he believes, 'for many thousand silent years.' It reveals its secrets only to those like himself who go into a trance, and 'dare for a time to join the dead.'

"He first brought me here when I was a boy. At that time, young and impressionable, I had an experience that could not come in middle age. I remember it vividly still. I felt great steps that shook the ground, and I heard my name called out. This was followed by an enormous laugh that echoed against the forest walls. In terror I cried, 'Who is there?' I heard old Kraychok muttering prayers, and the whole world grew suddenly dark... When I regained my consciousness, I was lying on the ground. He was slowly striking my head and repeating, 'All is well, little brother.' There was still a stern wild light in his eyes, but his voice was only sad and kind: 'You are too little to lie with the dead.'"

Again we were silent for some moments. Then Kraychok began to speak: "In old times, here was a famous place where foreigners came from the far seas. They brought heathen priests who were so wise they knew the darkest secrets. And here were done many bloody things, for they made human sacrifice. This woman's great womb was a flaming cave, and back to the mighty Mother of Life they gave the children she had borne. In this there was a fearful meaning. If a man lives, so too he must die. Do not think that what you see is only a granite figure—for in this spot many hundreds of mortals have shrieked and given their souls to God, and their spirits have never gone away. This is a place of mystery, where the deepest things in life have been born."

He stopped. He was standing rigid now. He went on in a voice intense and low:

"Any fool from the city coming here will feel his knees grow weak with fear, for there is something here that cries, 'Stop, you fool, and look into the depths of life and death beneath you.' Here this is plainly to be seen. But they do not know, these fools, that in all towns and cities, too, there are such ancient figures as these. Only there they are invisible. Men, who rush about in their haste and worry, over little things, have trampled such great figures down or buried them beneath the dust. But the souls of the figures still are there—even on busy city streets. They live still in the hearts of men. They only sleep. At times they rise, and then wild passions are let loose. In Petrograd is revolution; the street gutters flow with blood. And all over the world there is war today. The earth is black with armies, the winds are filled with voices—screaming, roaring. Guns, they say. But they are not guns." Old Kraychok's voice was soft and low. "They are the voices of great spirits, gods and devils, still alive in the hearts of men. So it is. And what will be the future nobody in the world can tell. For the future is a mystic thing, bound with iron to the past. And the past we do not understand.

"For there have been more people on the earth than drops of water in the sea. And they have found deep secrets, and the very deepest things have never been written down in books, for they were not found by the city men but by those who went alone under the sky even when the storm was dark, and into the blackest part of the forest even on the coldest nights. Such secrets have been handed down by a tongue that speaks to another ear—as I am speaking to you now." His voice was barely more than a whisper.

"But I can tell you little," old Kraychok ended sadly, "for I am one of the last of such men, and little has been revealed to me. All the world has turned to books and the deep things are forgotten. Now, for just a little while, the fools are frightened by what they see break loose in the wild years of war. But soon they will go back again to their books and little colleges."

Abruptly he turned from us. We followed him down the hummock and across the clearing. Back under the tall silent pines, he did not speak as he led the way. I was thinking of all that I had heard and of the huge symbol I had seen, of life endlessly renewing itself in agony and bloody sweat as Russia seems to be doing, these days.

"The future is a mystic thing, bound with iron to the past. And the past we do not understand."

# Chapter V

## 1

As I look back on the village now, the sorcerer looms in my memories as a stronger figure than the priest, but in the latter half of my stay, I came to know another man whose rugged force and vision of life made a still deeper impression. He was the school teacher. The weather-beaten frame house where he lived, with the blue paint nearly washed away by many Russian winters, stood on the high river bluff very close to the home of my friend. There he lived with his stout, good-natured wife and an old half-witted crone whom the neighboring peasants called a witch, but with whom the teacher was intimate friends. As a rule we found him working, mowing the hay in his small yard or sharpening his shining scythe, tinkering in his tool house or mending a fish net spread on the grass.

He wore a loose white cotton blouse, with a thick white cord at the waist. There were sandals on his feet, and a round cap of brown leather fitted close to the back of his head. He had small ears, a long powerful face with a receding chin and a heavy mustache, a high forehead, a long straight nose, and two little blue eyes that were still amazingly young. His voice, though harsh and guttural, was almost always very low, and as a rule he spoke rapidly. His hair was exceedingly soft and fine; it was brown with only a touch of gray. His face, his voice, and all his movements were like those of a man in his prime.

One day, when we went down to the river for our usual morning swim, we found him there before us; and the muscular strength in his lean brown body made me envy him his life. He dove like a youngster; with vigorous strokes he swam on his side out into the river, snorting and grunting. After our swim, we went up and had tea together. Later we went into the garden to sit on the grass and smoke cigarettes. Across the river, high up on a hill, stood the big school house he had built, dominating the neighborhood. It all comes back to me vividly now—the quiet garden, the fragrant breeze, the big black rooks in the trees above us. Little by little, we drew from the teacher the story of his work and life:

"I was born in 1865, some two hundred miles to the south of here, in a village about half-way between Petrograd and Riga. My father was a peasant, but he also kept the village store; and saving his money, bit by bit, he had at last acquired a farm of sixty-nine desiatinas (about 170 acres). I went to school in the village and later to the gymnasium (high school) in the town nearby. But I did not finish out my course.

Instead I went to Petrograd, to a training school for teachers. I graduated at eighteen, and since that time I have taught school in this province—for thirty-four years.

"In the first village where I taught, the peasants were hostile to the schools, as places where their children learned nothing of real use to the farm. But I thought, 'I will show how a school can affect the lives not only of children but parents, too, in practical ways. I will make my school the very heart and center of the neighborhood.'" The shrewd little blue eyes of the teacher twinkled reminiscently. "I had big thoughts when I was young.

"First of all, I wanted to prove to them the real profit to be had by learning to work together. And so, in a village near Schlüsselburg, I started a cooperative beehive association. I persuaded twelve peasants to try my plan. Each one put in a ruble to pay for the instruction, and each peasant bought one hive. We were successful from the start. One half the first year's profits was divided up among ourselves; the remainder went into the business. The government inspector of schools, who by good luck was a liberal man, noticed my work and gave me permission to extend it farther. I started small peasant cooperatives in orchards and vegetable gardens; and these, too, had a good success. Meanwhile, the children helped in the work, and so I taught them not only about gardens, orchards, and beehives, but also the value of cooperation. I made them see what miracles the bees could work by coming together in a hive. In our school garden, the second year, we grew strawberries nearly as large as eggs. The boys and girls grew absorbed in these jobs, they almost all worked hard for me, and so I had a splendid chance to mold their minds before they should harden and narrow into the ignorant ways, the sharp suspicions and jealousies that prevailed among the peasants there. I stayed in that village for many years.

"Then my friend, the inspector of schools, was replaced by a man who looked on me as a dangerous reformer. I was transferred to this neighborhood, to a school even humbler than the last. But here I started the same kind of work. The priest, Sergei Grigorovich, who had come some years before me, had already built his school in the village down the river; and he was prompt to give me his sympathy and good advice. I needed all that he could give, for the peasants were drunkards, a lousy lot, and the little school house to which I had come stunk like a pigsty in August. Gardening was impossible, for we had but a tiny plot of land. So I used some money of my own, and with the priest's help I took a lease on two desiatinas of land nearby. There we started our garden, our orchard, and our beehives. In the winter I taught the children from books; in the spring and summer we worked out of doors. And after three years of practical work, the attitude of the peasants toward the school began to change. I had kept some of the children with me there all summer long. Those from a distance lived with me. And now as they grew older they showed a knowledge of orchards and gardens that brought them excellent wages from the big landowners nearby. This made their parents approve of me.

## CHAPTER V

"I tried to give talks to the parents on modern farming methods and on cooperation. At first I did not have success, for they were still suspicious of all that came from the printed page. The revolution of 1905 brought a change in this attitude. Many peasant deputies were elected to the Duma then, and the people in the villages felt that they had a voice in the nation and must learn to use it well, in order to get the land reforms that they so hungrily desired. Many peasants began to learn to read and to look on books with more respect—but only on books that dealt with the land.

"Meanwhile there had grown up in my mind the dream of building a larger school, where in addition to class rooms there should be workshops of all kinds, to accommodate two hundred children. One day I had read in a paper of how in the United States they were building big school houses of this kind, even in new districts where as yet there were few children. That had given me my idea. And now, though I had little money, I began to make drawings for the new school. I had plenty of time to think out my plan, for it took me eight years to get money enough so that I could start to build. From my salary and from my school fund I saved about 300 rubles, and that was the beginning. I had some beehives of my own, and I used to sell the honey. Ruble by ruble the school fund grew.

"The priest, Sergei Grigorovich, was my greatest friend, those days. What a man of dreams he was, and how we schemed for the neighborhood! Long after midnight, sitting in bed reading a book or drawing my plans, I would hear a knock upon my door. For the tall ragged priest, striding over the fields from some hut where he had given the sacrament to a dying parishioner, and seeing the light in my window now, would drop in for a little talk. I would jump out of bed and open the door, and we would talk until daylight. The world sees few men with a genius like his. In twenty years he burned out his life—for that is the way with some Russians—but what light and warmth he shed around him, and what fun he had through it all! He was impatient of any delay. While pushing rapidly at that time the work on his small hospital, and a dozen things besides, he eagerly helped in the scheme for my work. In such night visits we would bend together over that plan of mine, and change it and figure and argue out our new ideas for a real school—'school of life,' he called it. Then he would stop for stories or jokes to drive home his arguments. And so the light of my lamp would fade, as the dawn came in through the window.

"He helped me in collecting funds. We drew up a subscription list, and I went through the district begging the land-owners and the merchants to subscribe. I pounded the idea into their heads. Some gave cash, and others promised building materials free of charge. I made several trips to Petrograd, and the Ministry of Education at last consented to grant me a credit of four thousand rubles. This caused a great sensation here and had at once a good effect. Our local iron merchant, who had promised three hundred rubles' worth of sheet iron and other material, now when he saw how our fame was spreading, agreed to raise his subscription to a thousand rubles. The priest had a hand in persuading him, and we two had a celebration that night.

"My friend the priest—how well he knew men!—gave me an excellent idea. It was to make use of the rivalry between our own big village and the one ten miles down the river. When our rival had started a fire brigade, we had at once responded by putting in electric lights—and now when they built a cinema theater, I urged that we must beat them by putting up a school house that would make them groan with envy. I organized a Building Committee, composed of all our leading lights. My Honorary Chairman was at first Prince C—, the Marshal of Nobility here; but later I decided to put some one else in his place. For I soon found it profitable to play upon the jealousies among these leading lights of ours. On the iron merchant I tried it first. One night, when he consented to open up a credit for another thousand rubles, I took the written agreement and added another zero very firmly to the sum; and when he stared at me dumbfounded, I leaned over and spoke to him in a confidential tone.

"The Marshal of Nobility is just about to resign as Honorary Chairman of the Building Committee,' I said. 'And I am almost certain that you are the one to take his place.'

"The merchant then swelled up with pride, for such a position would make his wife the first lady for miles around. It ended in his agreeing to leave on the extra cipher. Ten thousand rubles for the place of Honorary Chairman!

"Not long after that, I had a talk with another merchant here, who was planning to build a church. I made him see that a school house could do even more for God. I showed him how my plan would bring prosperity to the neighborhood, and how a grateful people would look up to the benefactors who had brought this change in their lives. Before I left, the merchant had promised an enormous sum.

"Then I went to the iron merchant, who was so furious at the news that he increased his own contribution, for as Honorary Chairman he felt that he must lead the list. He agreed to finish the whole job with his own money from then on, if in the principal room of the building his portrait could be hung on the wall with a motto underneath it to say, 'Here stands the creator of this school.' I knew that if I agreed to this scheme, the other donors would rise in a rage and ruin our plan. So I had to refuse his offer and go on begging smaller amounts.

"At last the building was finished. It was not what I had dreamed of, for the plans had changed from time to time according to the varying amounts of money we secured. It had taken eleven years in all, and I had written so many letters that once, when I weighed them just for fun, they tipped the scale at seven poods (thirty-seven pounds). Still, it had been a pretty good job.

"But then a joke was played on me. For I had built a school so large, the authorities in Petrograd decided that the head teacher here must be a very intelligent man with full university training. They got such a fellow, and I dropped out and went to a town some distance away, where I obtained a teacher's job more fitted to my standing."

## 2

This ended his first talk with us. We went to the school house that same day, but he did not offer to come along. High up on the bare hillside, it looked huge, crude, unfinished still; and after the story we had heard, it seemed to my eyes the mere shell of a school. The creating spirit was not there. It was empty, for this was vacation time, but we found the new principal installed in comfortable living quarters at one end of the building. The walls of his large living-room had been smoothly plastered, there was a rug upon the floor and white painted easy chairs. He himself was a little man with a rather pleasant affable face. He was dressed in a white duck suit with brass buttons on the jacket, the uniform of his government rank. He wore silver spectacles; he had a diminutive blond mustache. In a pleased contented way he talked to us about his work.

He had about ninety pupils of from eight to thirteen years of age. They were taught reading, writing, arithmetic, history and geography, "all under the rules prescribed in due form by the Ministry of Education." The teaching staff was composed of himself and three regular teachers, he said. The new priest in the neighboring village (the same little man with whom we had talked) came and managed religious instruction here in a most enlightened spirit. And besides, from the town nearby, special instructors came twice a week to teach singing, gymnastics, and drawing, and also French and German to the older pupils. In addition, there were in the basement two rough honest chaps of the peasant class, a blacksmith and a carpenter, who taught such work to some of the boys. This basement work had been the idea of a fine old country school teacher who had helped to build the school house, he said.

The pleasant little man talked on, but in spite of my efforts to listen to him, he kept melting away into thin air; and in his place there appeared in this room an uncouth figure, sinewy, brown, in a peasant's white blouse and a pair of old trousers, with sandals on his strong bare feet. I kept seeing his hairy throat and neck, burned by the sun in a life out of doors, his lean powerful face and shrewd blue eyes; and above all else, his long and narrow, muscular hands—with a jagged scar on the left wrist. He had broken that wrist while blasting out the cellar of this building.

## 3

Our second talk with him was at night. We came into his yard about nine o'clock, in the rapidly deepening dusk, and found him mowing with a scythe. He had been fishing that afternoon, and the long coarse net he had used was spread out on the grass to dry. We sat on a log bench under a tree. There was a chill of night in the air, but the teacher sat in his thin white blouse, which was open at his hairy chest, and with his bare sandaled feet in the tall grass now wet with dew, he appeared to me to be feeling particularly cozy. We spoke about the school house first.

"I hope those stoves in the class rooms are big enough," the teacher said. "I had planned a central heating plant in the basement, with steam boilers. This was to have run a dynamo, too, to supply the whole school with plenty of light in the dark days of winter. The man in charge was to have had the older boys as his helpers, and they would have learned from him at first hand about steam and electric power—so that when they grew to be men they would demand and know how to use the big steam tractors and other machines that we ought to have on all our farms. The Russians need to learn such things. I built that school in such a way that any room could become a shop. And I wanted special teachers there—blacksmiths, carpenters, plumbers, basket weavers, printers.

"This autumn," he continued, "I mean to start all over again, with a small agricultural school of my own. The school house will not be large, but instead of having the blacksmith there I shall send a few of my boys to the village blacksmith shop, and there they will learn better, because in a more practical way. Besides, it will interest them more. For almost any youngster will hang around a blacksmith shop, while if you bring the shop to the school, immediately it becomes a class, and the boy will soon begin to yawn. I shall send some boys to the carpenter, too. That is my new plan. A small school house, where we teach mainly the primary studies out of books; but all around, real shops and farms where the boys can work and earn money, and yet where I can have some control, and so inject little by little new methods, new tools and new machines into the work of the neighborhood. I want to do the same thing with the girls. There are some peasant women who are good cooks, and others who do fine sewing and weaving. They must be teachers for our girls."

While he was talking, every few minutes along the little country road peasant women, girls, and boys came by like ghosts, silently in their bare feet. Two passed in the semi-darkness now, and they had some children with them. The group went by without a sound, mere shadows moving in the dark.

"These people have so much in them," our friend continued softly, "things you would not notice, because they keep so much to themselves. But among them are natural teachers, and with their help I shall build my new school. How stupid it is to teach only with books. That of course is the easy way; for the peasants, having no faith in mere books, soon stop sending their children to school, so the work of the teacher is made light, and he can snooze the whole day long. But I think that the teacher, both day and night, should be the most wide-awake man in the village. The eyes of his spirit should never doze. He should do the hard thing; he should study the people, old and young, and find what is in them and build upon that.

"I want to dig the treasures not only out of the present here but out of the deep buried past. This neighborhood is a wonderful place for a teacher of real history. It was the very heart and center of our early Russian life. Wherever you dig you find old relics. I made a little start at such work. In certain places I knew about, I used to dig with the children. How hard they would dig! It was an adventure! Some days we would work far into the twilight. Bones and weapons, strange old tools, came out of the earth to reveal to us the life of the past. With these we started a museum. And I mean to start another one now, combined with a village library. Here, as they learn to dig in the ground, so too they will learn to dig in books, for the real, big treasures of the past. A teacher must be always there, whose job it shall be to give out books to the children and the parents alike. Many village libraries have been started in Russia of late years, but most of them simply give out books without studying the readers. And this is a stupid waste. The teacher should find what each reader wants, what kind of books appeal to him most, then plan a course to suit his needs, and so lead him slowly along the path—not a straight but a very crooked path, that goes winding up a hillside. For this is education.

"I should like to have lectures there at night, and classes for the parents, and cinema pictures every week, to spread a knowledge of foreign lands. Our peasants should learn of America. This is a most important point. Every school should teach English, every library should have a good stock of English and American books, to offset the ones that the Germans keep handing out as gifts to us. I tell you their agents have gone about for years to village libraries and schools. Those fellows are zealots; they work day and night. Have you no such zealots in your land? Why don't you send them over here? If you believe in liberty as the Germans believe in their devil's Kultur, you will come over by thousands and prove your belief by the things you do. You had a great man, Lincoln. You should make his story known in every Russian school house. Each time that a German speaks of his Kaiser, one of your people should be on the spot, to say, 'Now, brothers, let me tell you of a great American peasant. Abraham Lincoln was his name.'

"But stories will not be enough. It is practical work we need. There is no use in preaching to these Russian peasants. You must prove to them by actual deeds what progress and real science can do for their farms and villages.

"And the lack of such practical teaching is to blame for the state of our schools. What a scheme for popular education was started all over Russia in 1874! The Town Councils and the Zemstvos (district legislatures), composed of well-meaning liberal men, prepared a truly colossal plan, all done up in documents nicely tied with ribbons, a scheme for the education of every boy and girl in the land. But the funds were misused, and the amount for teachers' salaries was so low that the average teacher they secured was a poor specimen, dry as dust. Moreover, they taught the children only reading, writing, arithmetic. Nothing that would help on the farm. In the school house not a breath of life. And the peasants soon lost interest.

"Some of the peasants fiercely hoped for better lives for their children, and so they drove them still to the schools, in the hope that by all this scratching with pens they might learn to be volost (township) clerks. But seeing no such practical benefit to be had for the girls, the peasants kept their daughters at home. And by doing this, they held back the whole nation. For when you educate a boy it is only one man you are training, while when you instruct a girl you are molding a whole family—for everything that she has learned she will gradually teach to her children.

"So the work went limping on. A hundred million peasants—they called them muzhiks in those days, and our poor little Czar even called them that to the very time of his downfall. They were dirty, poor and ignorant, many of them soaked with drink; and few nice people would soil their hands by dipping into such a swamp. I remember the first school where I taught—the children with their rags and dirt, vermin, sickness, rotting teeth; they were always spitting and coughing about; you could hang an ax on the air in that room. So the well-to-do people kept away.

"Most of the Russian landowners were opposed to the very idea of such schools, for they wanted to keep the peasants down. In the dark old days of serfdom, their estates had been run by slave labor so cheap that they did not have to introduce modern farm methods or machines. And when at the Emancipation in 1861, the government of the Old Regime paid for each serf that was set free, the landowners wasted the money abroad, to such a degree that in foreign lands the very name of Russian came to mean a squanderer. This money paid to them for their slaves went into German health resorts founded expressly to cure Russians who had grown sick in Paris cafes. In the course of a generation most of our large landowners had become exceedingly poor. At the time of which I speak, they needed cheap labor on their estates in order to make two ends meet. And they were afraid that real peasant schools would raise the price of this labor.

"This was not true of all the landowners. Some were well-meaning, progressive men all bubbling over with ideals—but most of these chaps were impractical They spoke many fine words about education, but never took decisive steps to bring to the Russian peasant the knowledge that he needed in order to improve his life. The Zemstvos were almost wholly in the hands of such people as these. And although at the Zemstvo meetings there were a few peasant delegates, they were too abashed to speak in the presence of such fine company. They sat with their huge dirty beards pressed against the table, and only now and then did they show the indignation within them. This indignation would break out whenever any new plan was proposed for spending public money, for this money came mainly from taxes levied on the peasants themselves; and because the peasant delegates knew by sad experience how little benefit they received from any of these fine-sounding plans, they doggedly fought each new scheme which was to save humanity.

"The good of his own little neighborhood was all that each peasant cared for. His life was so hard that he had no time or wish to help make any improvement for the vast and unknown world which began for him a few miles from his hut. What a commotion would arise when there was talk of improving the roads! Every peasant delegate would sit there watching the map of the district, like an old wolf with keen gray eyes. If they talked of mending a road near his village, instantly he would shout for the scheme, and would try to drown out the hostile cries of the other peasant delegates for whom this road might just as well have been in a foreign land.

"And so, very little real work was done to improve the life of the neighborhood. All this affected the attitude of the peasants toward the schools. In brief, they were disgusted. They declared that by sending a boy to school you spoiled him as a laborer; and that if you sent your daughter there, you put such ideas into her head that often she went to the cities and towns where her body and soul soon rotted away. The first thing a girl did with her learning, they said, was to write love letters. That was the beginning, and God only knew the end!

"This was the general state of things when I started teaching school, over thirty years ago. Even then, there were many teachers and other idealists from the towns who had a glimmering of the truth that a school should teach the peasants things that would really better their lives. I had a little money, which my grandmother had left to me. This I used for the new ideas, of which I have already told you, and I was also able to try experiments outside. For example, I was able to help a good many poor devils who on account of their drunkenness were being sent as teachers to the loneliest village schools. I paid these chaps to send me reports as to what the peasants said about schools; and these reports I kept piling up, in order to strengthen by actual facts the appeal I intended to make later on to the government authorities.

"In one report a peasant said, 'Our teacher reads out of a book about how the dear little puppy dog died, and with this fine knowledge she sends out a boy to begin his life on the farm!' This was only one example of how the Russian peasants rebelled against the sentimental streak that ran through our school-books in those days. They had been drawn from German models, and the planners did not stop to think what a difference there is between German and Russian children. The Germans are sentimental; the Russians are realists to the core. And when these Russian children heard how the dear little puppy dog died, they showed nothing but disgust. Toward all such drivel, they themselves acted like young puppy dogs who are being dragged to a bath in the river. Doggedly they refused to dive into this German moonshine.

"As time went on, to the dry-as-dust reading, writing, arithmetic, the school authorities added many frills and furbelows, until the peasant in his disgust was even ready to return to the primitive schooling of the church. The priests skillfully took advantage of this, and started little parish schools which were still more badly run than were those of the Zemstvos. But the peasants felt that here at least, though nothing was done to lift their children out of wretchedness on earth, they were given instruction which opened the doors of heaven.

"So the work went blindly on. Since 1905, with the impetus the first revolution gave at that time, there has been a considerable speeding up and much has been accomplished. But nevertheless we are left to-day with the bulk of the problem facing us. How now can our schools be made centers of real education in all the useful ways and means by which a great free people shall raise its standards of work and life?

"As yet, the government has taken no important steps in this line. In the Ministry of Education there is a school committee, I hear, but I fear they are quite blinded by the long and elaborate program they are drawing up, in which the fundamental ideas are lost in a maze of detail. They should take on more practical men, fellows who come right out of real life—mining engineers, for example, and agricultural experts, and leaders from the large industries; because only with the aid of such men can there be drawn up a program which will meet our needs to-day. Instead of that, they plan to hold soon a colossal congress of teachers, and there will be so many specialists there that God knows what will come out of the storm. Round and round the ideas will go—like very dry leaves in a whirlwind!

"In the meantime, in the villages we must prove to the peasants the value of schools. The school I shall build will be very small. No more help from the government—I shall build it at my own expense, and so I shall have the freedom I need to make it exactly what I want. The wall space will be wholly free from portraits of benefactors. Instead of their dull faces, we shall have maps of America and other foreign countries, and pictures of fine model farms.

"For our school farm, we shall begin by draining the swamp in the hollow. I shall do this myself with the help of the boys. Next we shall clear the field of stones, and crush them up in a machine and fill the mud holes in the road. Then we shall plow and harrow well; and after we have sowed the field, we shall start a vegetable garden. Later on, an orchard. We must have some beehives, too; and as soon as we get time, I want to begin breeding fish in the river. We must have many kinds of work—for a child needs variety. To pull tough weeds in a garden all day is enough to kill his soul. We must have various kinds of jobs, and the child must be left to choose the ones that interest him most. But at the same time he must be shown that there is some work which nobody likes, and yet it is work that must be done, and in this each must bear his share. In brief, we must teach them to work in common, so that later as men and women they shall have deep in their souls the habit of true cooperation. For this is what the neighborhood needs."

Here the old teacher turned to Tarasov.

"I should like this little farm," he said, "to be a cooperative affair. Why not make it a part of that larger scheme of cooperative farming which you and I and those two peasants are planning to start? We can do it like this. I shall contribute this field of mine and the children will give their labor. You others will contribute the use of your horses and your farm machines and whatever added labor we need. And you and I and the children will then divide the produce. We must keep a strict account of our profits, for unless the peasants can clearly see the real advantage to be gained, they will never take our new idea. They must be shown just how much each field or garden cost us and exactly what is the yield. This, too, will be a fine thing for the school—for

I shall make the children learn to keep all such accounts, and so get the business training they need. Our books must be kept right up to date. Most Russian peasants keep no accounts, and so there is endless waste and confusion. We must teach the new generation the value of real management."

I had listened with deepening interest to the teacher's plan for a school, and now I began to tell him of similar schools in America. When I spoke of the experiment at Gary, Indiana, at once he was greatly excited.

"That's it—'the school of life'!" he exclaimed. "That is exactly the thing for us! It is what I have been working out. And now what a wonderful thing it is to hear that men in other lands have been traveling right along the same road! I tell you when this war is done, all the school teachers in the world must promptly get in touch with each other!"

He questioned me in close detail as to our new American schools, and when I could not give him the accurate knowledge he wanted, a hungry gleam came into his eyes. "I wonder how long it would take me to learn to read English," he said softly. "I must read all about this work myself. I do not want brief articles; I want to read whole books about it. I want to go through carefully the manuals used by the teachers themselves."

"You need not bother to read it in English," Tarasov interjected. "For my friend will send these books over to me from America, and I promise to translate them. I know a Russian publisher who will be glad to print such books, as soon as conditions settle down."

But the teacher shook his head.

"That might take two or three years," he rejoined. "And I am too old to wait so long. No, I shall tackle the job at once. This fall and winter I shall learn. Tell your friend that as soon as he sends the books I shall be able to read them. And with their guidance you and I must plan out this whole experiment. Of course we must not blindly swallow the American scheme; we shall take from it only what is adaptable to our Russian life."

"Why don't you make your plan international?" I suggested. "Let me put in a few hundred rubles and become the American partner in your new cooperative school."

When this was translated, the teacher leaped up and warmly gripped my hand in his. The silver spectacles dropped off his nose, and swung by their black cord at his waist, as with rapid gestures he talked in his low guttural voice:

"This is the last stone we needed! Now we can lay the foundations at once! I have already talked to those two other peasants, and I am sure they will come in. How much longer will your American friend be here?" he asked of Tarasov. And when the latter told him that I was to leave the following day, the old man rose abruptly.

"Then, gentlemen, goodnight!" he cried. "It is my wife who owns this land, and she has the money, too. I must not let her get to sleep; I must talk this out with her at once! Tomorrow I shall come to you ready to do business!"

## 4

The next day bright and early he appeared.

"I have talked to my wife half the night," he announced, "and everything is settled. We have decided to call it The Cooperative Farming School. In place of our old cabin we shall build a good strong house of logs for ourselves and the school children. I could not sleep, so at sunrise I went to those two peasants, and they have agreed to contribute labor, horses, plows, and tools. You shall do the same, and your friend from America shall put in some money. A very little will suffice. Let him hold one of our twenty shares—just enough to prove to us the interest of his country. That will have a value here—for I know these peasants well, and as soon as the word goes around that we have an American partner, they will begin to nod their heads and say, 'This is a big thing, brothers.' And they will all be trying to get their children into our school. The local village merchants will grow quite green with envy. But we will not take their money. We want no benefactors here!"

"Still," I proposed maliciously, "if I am to be a partner, don't you think you might hang up in the school a good big American portrait"—I paused, and the teacher eyed me with sharp uneasiness and dismay—"of Abraham Lincoln?" I ended. Instantly his expression cleared.

"Excellent! We shall do it!" he cried. He talked rapidly on of his plans for the school.

"We must take very few pupils at first—about thirty at the most," he said. "Some of them shall live with us, for my wife and I are childless and we are both getting old; we want to see a crop of children growing right before our eyes. So we shall keep them here all year. In the winter we shall study from books, and the rest of the year we shall work in the fields and in the woods and down on the river." The teacher rose abruptly.

"I tell you," he cried, "if such education years ago had been spread all over this country, there would not have been any war or any need of a revolution. There would have been steady growth instead, a steady rise in well-being and intelligent ways of work that would have put our people far on the road to real freedom. And Russia would have been so strong that Germany would not have dared to start this war of conquest. For our country is as large as all the rest of Europe combined, and as a free intelligent people, we could have had the strength of a giant, so tall that his head is in the clouds!

"As it is, we must do our utmost to help defeat the Germans now. We who see the danger must make our neighbors see it, too. 'War or slavery,' we must say. No matter what confusion, shame, and ruin shall befall—the whole nation toppling down—still we must work on and on. 'War or slavery!' we must say, in every village, every hut—until at last the peasants rise. The German autocracy must be gripped, and slowly, slowly choked to death. It will be a long job, brothers. You Americans must understand that you have years of blood before you, and that whether you win or lose will depend on whether Germany can recruit her armies here. We have twelve million fighting men. Two million may decide this war—one, two, three years from now. Who shall get them? You or Germany? That decision rests with you.

"If I were an American I would say, 'By the love of Christ and Liberty, these Russians shall be made our friends. By our deeds we will make them understand.' The German agents tell us here, 'The Americans are money hogs. They have joined with England in this war to build a world power that shall grab all the richest lands of the earth. They want to make you fight their war while they crush your revolution, so that their millionaires may be free to go on with their looting of mankind.' Such lies are being believed by our peasants, who are blind and weary of war. Remember we have already lost three million killed, and two million more of our young men have died of starvation and disease. Be patient, friendly, careful, kind. Think long and hard—but not too slowly—plan your deeds; then act like men. You must act in such a way that while you fight the Germans among us, you will make us understand that you are our brothers, with no wish to interfere with our will to be free. Brothers of liberty you must be. Only so can the war be won.

"And after that, education!" The teacher's low voice was so intense that it trembled a little in spite of him. "Education all over Russia," he said. "And then no more bloody wars in the world. For in twenty years we shall have at least two hundred million people here, and they will all be for keeping the peace. They will be as your people have been too busy with their inner growth to be seeking foreign quarrels. The work of developing our country, which is one-sixth of the earth, and the work of developing so many people, so many children's growing minds—I tell you it is staggering. And it would be a crime if we let ourselves be blind and think it can soon be done. It may take generations.

"I'll tell you one of the plans I have. It is to organize all the boys in companies and regiments. This was once tried by Peter the Great, but only to make them slaves of his rule, and that is not my plan at all. I would plant in their minds the great idea of marching, fighting, and working together in a great free brotherhood, which when it spread to other lands would be a tremendous force in defense of the liberties and the peace of mankind."

"It has begun already," I said. I began to tell him of the Boy Scouts in England and America. And as he listened in growing surprise, his lean wrinkled powerful face grew boyish in its eager delight.

"What a thing it is!" he cried huskily. "War is bad, a curse on the earth; and yet how it smashes open our minds! Here, for years in our village, I have been thinking out a plan, and now I find it has been growing in other men's minds all over the world! All right, brothers, so much the better! Now what shall we talk of? What next, my friends?"

He began to walk excitedly. Presently with an anxious frown he sat down again on the grass.

"But remember, this is no time," he said, "for us to get excited, and blind to the actual state of things. It is all very well to make fine plans—but what have we got to build on? Now I shall try in a businesslike way to tell you how the people feel so that your country may know the truth.

"At the start of the revolution, the peasants in this district prepared to take over all the land of the private owners. And they said, 'We shall not pay them a kopeck. These fine barins robbed and exploited us for generations. Now it is our turn, brothers. We shall no longer waste our strength pushing our bellies against the lever to pull up stumps from unused ground. We shall take the rich lands of the barks themselves!' I said to them in answer:

"'No injustice of the past can be righted by mere robbery now. The job is not so simple. Surely you must get more land, and the barins must give up what you need. But let us take time to find a way by which it can be thoroughly done. Let us make a good job of this.'

"Some of the peasants listened and grew more moderate in tone. And since then more and more of them have come around to my point of view. For they know I don't care for my own little life. I have little more land than the average peasant, and what I have, I shall gladly devote to this school farm of which I spoke. But I care very much for the common good; and if in their present ignorant state, the peasants should seize the land from the owners, half of it would suffer from lack of good cultivation, and so the crops would soon decrease and there would be terrible famine here. And I say this must not be. Before they are fit to own all the land, the peasants must learn two great things. First, they must be taught modern farming—how to get the most out of the soil; and second, every one of them must learn to work for the good of all. At present they are as suspicious of each other as gray wolves. By the right kind of teaching they must be shown what the revolution means. It means that every one must be made happy and satisfied with his life; that instead of dragging down those at the top, the lowest must be brought right up, by education and practical help.

"There must be no difference made in our schools between the children of peasants and those of any other man. The school must be a meeting ground and draw all the children of Russia together. They cannot start too soon to be friends. Every school must be made so good that no gentleman will think it unfit for the education of his child. To do this, we shall be forced to spend hundreds of millions of rubles a year—but it will be a rich investment! For from such schools there will grow up a new generation of people—schoolmates, brothers, every one!

"I believe that the people should own all the land. Let them little by little take it away from those who now have more than enough. And meanwhile our new government should introduce heavy taxes upon capital of all kinds, that will slowly, year by year, cut into private fortunes and so lead to equality. But the money taken from the rich must be used to so raise the level of all, that the rich will not suffer by the change—except to lose their snobbishness, which is the very worst thing that they own.

"Now is the time for such fellows as us to work day and night, to prove to the peasants that we are workers like themselves, and that, while we want them to have more land, we are also searching for better ways by which they can get more out of the soil with less labor than at present. For that, we must have modern machines the very best." He turned to Tarasov abruptly.

"The last time that you were here, you spoke of a farm tractor. How much would such an engine cost?"

"Six thousand rubles," Tarasov replied.

"I'll put up half," said the old man promptly.

"I'll try to raise the rest," I said, "and I'll try to have the tractor sent over from America." The teacher leaned forward eagerly.

"You must do it," he cried, "and do it soon! For I tell you when that great steel horse comes up the river on a barge, it will cause such excitement here that all thought of rioting will disappear. Even now I can shut my eyes and see that mighty engine forging along the river banks, plowing not only the arable soil but also opening up new fields by tearing through bushes and small trees. And I see the silent peasants watch, with a deep excitement in their eyes. We must not be too eager to show we wish to help them. No benefactor poses here. We must just go about our business, and not until they come and say, 'Please bring your tractor to our fields,' shall we offer to plow their land. We shall charge them exactly what it costs. Then we shall say, 'Why don't you save your money instead of paying us for this? It is good business, brothers. Gather your neighbors and raise a fund and buy an engine just like ours.' So we shall spread cooperative groups, and meanwhile we shall work out the whole plan of farming the land in common.

"The main danger will come from Berlin. The Germans will never leave us alone; for their rulers know that if they allow us to grope our way through the darkness now, we shall reach a day of freedom so splendid and so dazzling that it will flood Europe like the sun—and autocracy will slink from the earth. And so, as they have done in the past, they will try to put us Russians down, and keep us a nation of muzhiks—slaves on our farms, to feed them in their towns. There are hundreds of thousands of Germans here, but you cannot show me one who has ever tried to do anything to improve our village life. They have always tried to make friends with the merchants in our cities, in order to exploit the peasants. And if they now force a conqueror's peace, you may be sure that it will be at the expense of the villages.

"The man is blind who does not see that blood must flow in Russia still. Never mind what they do in Petrograd. We shall not make peace with that gang in Berlin. If they come and try to take our grain, we will fight, I tell you, we will fight—not in a great army but in small bands of resolute men who know the country, know where to hide in the forest and where to strike from the high river bank. We shall be like wasps all over Russia, stinging those big German hogs when they come and try to root out the food which we have hidden in the ground. They will be forced to take by violence all the grain they get from us, and they will do such murder here as will put an end forever to any chance of our friendship so long as the Kaiser rules in Berlin.

"So we shall go on—through to the end. But at last when the war is won, we must do much more than that. We must find out all the things that have made the Germans strong, both the good and the bad. The bad we must uproot from the world, but all that is good we must hold as tight as a man grips his plow upon rough ground—for only so can we make the earth rich to yield a new life for the children. I speak not of Germany alone. We must get the good from all countries, especially from their villages.

"In this village I watch the people. I see them pass along the road. I look down on the river—the boats go by. And I feel a deep strong power here. It is the power of daily life. It has been strained to the breaking point in the big towns and cities, but out here in the villages the daily life of men goes on. It is like a vast reservoir containing all that men and women have done day and night for thousands of years—what they have wanted, hoped and dreamed. And this is what we must build on.

"It is time for every one of us, no matter how weary he be from the war, to take a fresh start and ask, 'What can I do?' I myself am a country teacher. There must be millions of us in the world, and every teacher among us, I say, must watch his people closely and try to help them climb a hill where they can see out over the earth. This is hard for them to do. Their lives are cramped. They live in small huts, and at work in their fields they keep their eyes upon the ground. So they have near-sighted souls. But even among such people, I watch and I see that most of them, driven by a mysterious force which seems to have risen in this war, every now and then climb the hill and try to see the villages that are scattered over the world. And so I believe it is in all lands. Out of their huts the peasants go, and when they have reached the top of the hill, they scowl in the blinding sun up there. And they ask:

"'Where are you, brothers? And what have we done, in the name of Christ? Why have we killed each other? What did we want down there in the darkness? To kill each other? Not at all, for it is a foolish business. We were driven to it like sheep, by the crime that was started in Berlin. Now it is time to rise like men, and talk together, find out what we really want. We want better lives, more food and clothes and better huts and finer schools for our boys and girls. You must tell us how you live and work—all your latest tricks in farming, all your latest tricks in schools. We must see each other clearly, and we must find how to stop all wars. Not by a whirlpool of chatter like that going on in Petrograd, but by hard slow work and learning, we must climb the long road to a better world.'

"I say that the teacher can help them learn. But to be successful, he must not try to climb too often to the heights. He must stay down in the village, help the peasant mend his plow and help the housewife mend her stove, and work and live every day with the children. For only when the teachers live deep down in the life of the people can we ever dare to hope that the people will climb up the hill. For I tell you we must look ahead with clear eyes and steady nerves; we must set to work in a practical way—and basing all our planning on the power of daily life, which flows like a great river underneath the storm of this war, we must build a new world through the children—so slowly that you will never be able to say to yourself, 'Now it is here.'"

## 5

The teacher stopped, and for a few moments nothing was said. Then he looked up with a scowl of annoyance. The many rooks in the trees overhead were making a terrific noise.

"Let us leave these devils," he proposed, "and go into the house."

We went into Tarasov's workroom. There the old man laid hold of a plow and began to examine it closely. He questioned Tarasov about it and for some minutes they grew absorbed, while I used the time to fill in my notes. Then I asked him many questions about the war and the village life. We talked for several hours more. When we had lunched, I left them and went for a stroll up the riverside. When I came back they were still there.

Our departure for the city was put off to the following day.

The next morning we rose early, breakfasted and packed our bags. We had arranged with a peasant to bring his dory and take us out to the small river steamer when it came by. But now when we looked down from the bluff there was no dory to be seen, and we could already hear the steamer tooting for the village landing a little over a mile away. Tarasov hurried off for a dory, while I took my bags and went down the steep path.

On a raft of logs moored to the bank, I saw a small ragged boy who was fishing. Then I spied the teacher coming down from his cabin on the bluff nearby, with a towel on his arm, for his morning swim. He went out to the urchin on the raft and sat down beside him, drew up the line and examined the bait, then let it drop back. The next moment he caught sight of me, and jumping up eagerly he called out,

"You are just in time for a last swim!"

We proceeded quickly to undress. I remember the teacher's long lean body, muscular, brown, as he poised on the log. Then he dove, and with long over-head strokes swam out into the river, where he turned over on his back and blew like a porpoise. In a few moments, all aglow, we were dressing in the crisp cool air. Tarasov came hastily down the bluff with his enormous bag on his shoulders. A dory put out from the opposite bank, and the steamer came puffing around the bend. The dory reached us just in time. We threw in our luggage. Then I turned back, and the teacher warmly grasped my hand.

"Remember that you are to come again."

"Yes, I'll come," I promised him.

"And in your country, tell them—no matter what happens, *remember us—the people in the villages*!"

"I'll try to tell them."

Already we were out in the stream. The steamer approached and slowed down to half speed. We threw a rope to a deck hand, who made it fast for a moment, while with our bags we clambered up; and the steamer forged ahead. Behind us, on the raft of logs, the teacher was standing motionless, with his towel upon one arm. Catching sight of me, he started to wave—but then he turned back suddenly. For the urchin beside him gave a shrill cry. He had hooked a fish—a big one! The teacher helped him pull it in.

## **THE END**

# INDEX

"A Club" xiv
Addams, Jane xi
Admiralty 23
Agricultural machines 20–22; hopes for from America 29
Amalgamated Meat Cutters and Butcher Workmen of North America xii
America, agricultural implements 22, 29; dances from 51; interest in 63
American Federation of Labor xii
American Red Cross xvi, xviii
Archangel 53
Armour, Philip Danforth ix
Artillery Board 23
Astrakhan 53
*Avalanche* xix

Beattie, Bessie xvii n42
*Beggars' Gold* xix
Berlin xiii, xvi, 3, 31, 109–10
*Blind* xix
"Bloody Sunday" xiii
Board of Explosives 23
Bolsheviks 1, 53
*Bookman* ix
Boston iv n27
Bowery YMCA xix
Breckinridge, Mary xx
*Bridge, The* xx–xxi
Brook Farm 29
Brooklyn vi
Brubaker, Howard xi, xiv
Brusilov, Alexei Alexeevich 4, 4n3, 44, 48
Brusilov offensive 48, 84
Buddhists 82
Buffalo Bill's Wild West Show xiii
Bullard, Arthur x, xiv–xix

Cahan, Abraham xi
Carpathians 44, 84

Catholics 81–82
Caucasians 53
Caucasus xiii–xiv, xiv n24–xiv n25
Charcot, Jean-Martin 87, 87n2
Chekhov, Anton xiv n27
Chicago ix–x, xiv n27, xv, xviii, xx; book about xx–xxi; Board of Trade ix; north side ix
*Chicago Tribune* xii
China 6
Chinamen 6-7
Chirikov, Evgenii xiv n27
*Chosen People, The* xiv n27
*Collier's Weekly* xi
Committee for Public Information xvii–xviii
Commons, John xii
Cooperative plan 39
Cooperative Farming School 106
Cooperative Society. *See* Village Cooperative
Cossacks 12, 19
Country doctor's views 11–12
Creel, George xvii, xix
Creel Committee xvii
Czar's abdication 23

*Dark People: Russia's Crisis, The* xviii
Darrow, Clarence x
Denmark 22
Depression xix–xx
Donnelly, Michael xii
Duma 97

Education 106–08
Edison, Thomas 83
Emancipation, Peasant 11, 102
England 21–22, 81
Eve of St. John's Day 88–89

Far East xii, 35
Finland 69

Finnish girl 65–66, 68; aspires to study medicine 69–72
Finns 3, 53; in Tarasov's village 14, 16–17, 35, 65–66, 75
Ford, Harriet xv, xv n31
Ford car 24
Foreign Press Bureau xix
France xvi, 21–22, 81
Franconia xix, xxi
Freedom of Religion 82
French Revolution 71
Frontier Nursing Service xix
Frost, Robert xx

Galician offensive, 1916 4n3
Garland, Hamlin xvi
Gary, Indiana 105
Georgia ix
Georgians 4
Germans 59, 64, 103, 106
Germany xvi, 11, 21–22, 47, 71, 106–07
*Giants Gone: Men Who Made Chicago* xx
Gorky, Maxim ix, xiv n27, xx
Grandfather Front 45
Great Northern Hotel, Petrograd 25
Great Revolution 10
*Great White Hills of New Hampshire, The* xxi
Great War xx
Greenwich Village xv, xx
Guards (regiments) 24, 49, 51
Gypsies 4

Hackett's Theater xv
*Harbor, The* xvi, xxi
Hard, William xii
Harper, William Rainery xii n15
Haymarket Square Riot, 1886, Chicago xii
Haywood, Bill xx
Henry, O. xx
Henry Street Settlement, New York x–xi
Hermitage (art gallery) 24–25
*His Family* xvii
Hitler, Adolph xx
Holy Saints 90
Howells, William Dean xvi, xx
Hull House, Chicago x–xii
Hungarian prisoners 67
Hungary 4, 48
*Hunter's Moon* xix

*Independent* xiv
Inflation 12n6, 43, 46
Italy xx, 41

Japan xii–xiii
Jewish immigrants x
Jewish revolutionaries 11
Jewish Theater, xi
Jews 81–82
July Days, or Insurrection xviii, 1, 43

Kaiser 31, 48, 101, 110
Kennan, George xi n14, xiii
Kentucky xx
Kerensky, Alexander 1–2, 60
Kerensky offensive, 1917 4
King, Fred xi
Kishinev xiv n27
Kittredge, Mabel xv
Kraychok, village sorcerer 85–93, 95; as hunter 88

Ladoga Lake 90
Lake Forest ix–x
Lake Michigan ix
Lincoln, Abraham 101, 106
Lippmann, Walter xvi
Liteiny (Petrograd street) 24
Local noble landowner 13, 16–17
London 3, 62
Long, Robert Crozier xvii n42
Lower East Side, New York x–xii
Lukanina, Adelaide (Paevskaia) 69n2
Lutherans 81–82

Macmillan, publisher xvi, xix–xx
*Manchester Guardian* xiii
Manchuria xiii
"Marseillaise" 28, 31
*McClure's Magazine* xi
McDowell, Mary xi–xii
Michigan Avenue, Chicago ix
Mir 37–38, 37n1, 38n2
Mohammedans 81–82
Moscow ix, 1, 10–11, 19, 25n9
Munich xii, xv
Mussolini, Benito xx

# INDEX

*Nancy Flyer: A Stagecoach Epic, The* xxi
Navy Board 23
Nazimova, Olga xiv n27
Neighborhood Guild, New York x
Neva River 2
Nevsky Prospect, Petrograd xvii, xviii n43, 4, 25
New Hampshire xv, xx–xxi, 9
New York, city xx–xxi, 3, 39, 62; state ix
New York Charity Organization Committee xi
*New York Times* xix, xxi
Nicolaevsky station 25, 25n9
Nicholas II 26, 91n3
*None So Blind* xv
Novgorod 52
*Nurses on Horseback* xx

Old Believers 82
Old Regime 24–25, 27, 79, 82–83, 102
Orlenev, Pavel Ivanovich xiv, xiv n27
Orthodox Church 81–83, 83n1
Ostrovsky, Alexander 67, 67n1
*Outlook* ix, ix n14, xi, xiii–xiv

Paris xiii, xvi, 18, 20, 62, 87
Pasteur, Louis 83
Peasant Emancipation 11
Peasant fishermen 13; landholders 11
Peasants' Council 41–42
Peking xviii
Pennsylvania 84
People's Bank, Moscow 57
People's House, in village 58, 63, 68
Petrograd xviii, 1, 4, 6–7, 13, 24, 33, 62, 68, 77, 85; agitators from 16–17; criticism of soldiers in 59–60; February/March revolution in 22–25; Fine Arts Academy 20; Germans in 27; grandmother's marriage in 19; Jews in 11; Lutheran school in 69, 72; Medical University in 19, 69; news from 10; resentment of in countryside 30, 39, 46, 59–60; restaurants in 2; violence in revolution 92–93
Poole, Abram (father) ix
Poole, Abram (artist brother) xii, xv
Poole, Bertha (sister) x
Poole, DeWitt Clinton ix n1

Poole, Ernest, American writer ix, xi, xix, 64; autobiography xx; Committee for Public Safety xix; education of x–xi; death of xxi; marriage xv; journalist in Russia xvi–xvii; knowledge of Russian 69; novelist xvi–xvii, xix, 22n8; on river steamboat 8–11; on train to village 7–9; Revolution of 1905 xiii–xiv; theater interests xiv–xiv n27; visit to Tarasov's village 16 *et passim*
Poole, Frederick C. ix n1
Poole, Margaret (wife) xv–xvi, xxi
Poole, Ralph (brother) xv
Poole, William (son) xxi
Port Arthur xii–xiii
Prince C— 13, 16–18, 35, 58; as Marshall of Nobility 98
Princeton University x
Prohibition, alcohol 53, 53n8
Provisional Government xviii, 81, 104; Minister of Agriculture of 28–29, 32; Ministry of Education of 81, 97, 99, 104; Minister of Railroads of 31
Pulitzer Prize for fiction xvii
Pullman Strike, 1894, Chicago xii
Pushkin, Alexander, quoted 26

Rasputin, Grigory 91n3
Red Guards 1–2
Reed, John xvi–xvii, xvii n42
Revolution of 1905 1n1, 97, 103
Riga 95
Rome 71
Roosevelt, Theodore xv–xvi
Russia, destiny of 35, 47; a new Russia 48
Russian Revolution, 1917 ix; 1905 ix, 2
Salvation Army Hotel xix
*Saturday Evening Post, The* xvi–xvii, 3n2
Sawmill owner 49–51
Schlusselburg 96
Scott, Leroy x
Sergei Grigorovich, village priest 74–77, 96–98
Shepherd, William, journalist xvii, xvii n42
Sherman, William Tecumseh ix
Siberia xviii, 84
*Silent Storm* xix
Silesia xvi
Sinclair, Upton xii

Singer sewing machines 44, 44n5
Sisters of Mercy (Russian Red Cross) 76, 78
Soviet of Soldiers and Workers 31
"St. Petersburg Players" xiv n27
St. Petersburg University xiii
Starosta (village elder) 57
Steamer, river 8, 13, 111–12
Steffens, Lincoln xi
Stockyards Strike, Chicago xi
Stokes, Phelps x
Stolypin, Petr, chairman of council of ministers 22n8
Stolypin reform 22n8, 37n1, 42
Sugar Hill xix, xxi
Swede 22, 75

Tarasov, Ivan (Juvenale's father), painter's studio 14, 56, 86; becomes a village farmer 21, 45; death of (1911) 21; student in Fine Arts Academy 20
Tarasov, Juvenale (Iuvenalii Ivanovich) xiii, xviii, xxi–xxii; 1n1; as chemist 23 becomes village farmer 21–22; biography of 21–33; critical of American speed 5, 49; French grandmother 18–19; French library 18; grandmother 86–87; house described 14; leaving Petrograd 1–3; on train and steamer to village 6–13; passion for farming 14, 21–22; promotes agricultural reform 37; with storekeeper 56; travels in Europe 22; village described 13–15, 20, 36, 40, 45; visit to his mother in Petrograd 26–27; witness of February/March revolution 23–30
Tarnopol, Russian retreat from (1917) 12, 40
Tatars 4, 53
Tauride Palace 31
Thompson, Donald xvii n42
Tokyo xviii
Tolstoy, Leo ix–xi
Transportation problems 46, 46n6
Trans-Siberian Railroad xiii, xviii, 6, 9
Tsushima, Battle of xiii
Turgenev, Ivan ix–x
Tyrkova-Williams, Ariadna xiii n19

Ukrainians 53
*Uncle Tom's Cabin*, Harriet Beecher Stowe 67
Union Army ix

Union of Cooperatives 57, 61
United Press xvii
United States, school-houses in 97
University of Chicago x; Settlement House xi
University of Wisconsin xii
University Settlement, New York x–xi, xii n15
*Up From Slavery*, Booker T. Washington 1

Vanderpoehl ix
*Village: Russian Impressions, The* xiii, xviii–xix
Village Cooperative 57, 60, 62; builds People's House 63
Village, described 14–16, 20–22, 36–37, 56–57; departure from 111–12; drunkenness in 73–74, 76; elections in 39–40; Hungarian prisoners in 67, 84; hospital in 62, 78; midwife in 62; priest in 74–81, 87, 96; school house in 64–65, 72, 75, 99–100; school teacher in 64, 73, 87, 95–100; storekeeper in 56
Vladikavkaz xiv
Vladivostok xii
*Voice of the Street* xi
Volga 53
"Volga boatmen" 53n7
Voltaire 19, 86

Wald, Lillian xi, xx
Walling, William English x, xiv
Washington, Booker T. 1
Washington Square, New York xiv
Wells, H. G. xi
Western Front xvi
Weyl, Walter (brother-in-law) x, xiv
White, William Allen xvi
White Mountains xvi, xix
Williams, Harold xiii, xiii n19
Wilson, Woodrow x, x n5, xx
Winter Palace xviii, 2, 24–25
Winterbotham, Katherine xv
Winterbotham, Margaret Ann x, xv
Wisconsin ix
*With Eastern Eyes* xix
Woman's City Club, New York xv
Women's Battalion of Death 70
Women's Medical College of Pennsylvania, 69n2
World War I 3n2, 70n3; effects of 40, 40n3
World War II xxi

World's Fair, 1893 ix

Yankees 49

Zemstvo, district assembly 12, 59, 101–03

www.ingramcontent.com/pod-product-compliance
Lightning Source LLC
Chambersburg PA
CBHW032028230426
43671CB00005B/235